SOUL GRAFT

BRAD HILL

COVENANT PUBLICATIONS
Chicago, Illinois

ISBN 0-910452-66-0
Copyright © 1988 by Covenant Publications

Design: *David R. Westerfield*
Cover Photo: *Brad Hill*
Production: *Susan Miller, Jane K. Swanson-Nystrom,
Debra Almgren, Gregory Sager*

Covenant Publications
3200 West Foster Avenue
Chicago, Illinois 60625
(800) 621-1290, (312) 478-4676

CONTENTS

PREFACE

How is the Church to bear the revelation of God through Christ to the world? Jesus said, "Peace be with you. As the Father has sent me, even so I send you" (John 20:21). Jesus sets himself as the model of our mission.

Our understanding of the Church's ministry is conditioned by how we see the ministry of Jesus. Jesus embodies the revelation by his life as the Servant and the Son of man, identifying with humanity while pointing to God.

If identification with those to whom we minister is the catalyst of missions, then our participation in their lives is the authenticating sign of God's love.

In this book I want to share my own pilgrimage—as well as my family's—on the way to such identification in multiple cultures. Some of the details of these stories have been altered for reasons of continuity and privacy, but in the broader sweep they represent faithfully our own experience as missionaries to Africa. We hope they will also make you, the reader, more sensitive to the challenge of following and representing Jesus wherever he leads.

To my wife, Ruth,
who lives the stories with me . . .

PART ONE
LEAVING ON A JET PLANE

*Tears and hugs in the airport are
the currency of departure and reflect
the anguish of separation.*

PERSPECTIVE

The hardest sacrifice any missionary makes is leaving family and friends. No matter how well you prepare yourself for separation and adaptation, there is a stab of sadness when the time comes. As the day approaches, hilarious laughter and intimate moments are programmed into the memory. These will be needed resources for the years ahead.

A positive response to the call of God for living and working and raising a family in an adopted culture is a mixed blessing. The initial idealism of missionary work wears off, and it becomes important to know why you are where you are—probably not doing what you thought you would be doing.

My own journey of call has progressed through three stages which give perspective to my motivation and a reason to endure. Hearing the call as *commandment* forces us to wrestle with the issues of obedience and priorities. "Go therefore and make disciples of all nations" (Matthew 28:19). The commandment, which initially intimidates, gives way to *compulsion*. We are driven by the Holy Spirit, and "Woe to me if I do not preach the gospel" (1 Corinthians 9:16). Finally, the call brings us to *compassion*. Our need for a needy world is accentuated; our conviction that there is a universal need for the Gospel is steeled. Compassion for the people produces an acute sense of personal unworthiness and inability. We depend on the reality of God's grace in our lives.

Tears and hugs in the airport are the currency of departure and reflect the anguish of separation. To the extent the roots run deep, the transplantation is difficult; and we wonder whether it is worth the sacrifice and separation. But the words of Paul ring strong and true: "Indeed I count everything as loss because of the surpassing worth of knowing Christ Jesus my Lord. For his sake I have suffered the loss of all things, and count them as refuse, in order that I might gain Christ" (Philippians 3:8, NIV).

ONE

BEN TOLLS
FOR ME

As was my custom, I arrived early at the First Church, which was the last church on my furlough itinerary. Soon our family would leave for Africa for the third time. The door was unlocked, but nobody was around. I entered timidly and looked around while unburdening myself of Bible, literature on Africa, slide projector and screen, extension cords, and boxes of slides for the evening service. Methodically, I moved into action, removing the guest book from its place on a card table and spreading out my pamphlets. I had done this a hundred times, but this would be the last stand before our departure the next week. Having nothing further to occupy my mind, I stood around the narthex practicing my nonchalance. I felt as alone and out of place as Amos the shepherd felt before Amaziah. Plush sofas lined the wall, and a glass-walled garden beautifully decorated the narthex.

I am glad for literature racks. They provide visitors with a place to stand, an excuse for being there, and something to do with their hands if not their minds. I rifled through the tracts and old Sunday school handouts. Bulletins from past services were stuffed into the slot with the offering envelopes, many of which sported the impressionistic doodlings of bored children. One drawing resembling a cross between Santa Claus and the devil was entitled "pastor." I pawed through them, finally finding the bulletin from the last Sunday. There it was! My name in print! "Bard Hill from China will be with us for our yearly missions Sunday. Potluck following." Parishioners must be enticed with promises of food before they come to hear a missionary.

Above the literature rack hung a creased pre-Copernican map of the world with little red pins on it. Each pin represented a stuck missionary. The pin in my area had fallen out. Surrounding the map were pictures of missionaries taken in the late fifties.

Noticing the door entitled "Gentlemen," I suddenly needed to use the facilities. I went in and the door swung shut behind me with a pneumatic sigh. I groped for the switch where it should have been but wasn't. Continuing to stumble around in the dark, I came to the sink and so decided to wash my hands instead. Still playing blind man's bluff, I felt along the wall to the door again. Ah! There was the switch behind the door. I came out into the narthex again. Still alone.

The carpeted hall led me towards the sanctuary. Loneliness shadowed me as I wandered around this church edifice. A single strain from a popular sixties song hummed inside my head, "One Is the Loneliest Number." Church crowds usually accentuate my singleness, and the anguish of isolation increased as the departure for Africa neared.

Within a few minutes cars would arrive and disgorge children and chicken casseroles tucked under the arms of well-dressed parents. They would come streaming through the double doors—talking, laughing, glad to be home. An official greeter would post himself at the door and say how glad he was to see everyone. He would have a hearty handshake. They would all know one another, but they would not know me. Once again I would have to find a way to tell them who I am and determine who they are.

The sanctuary was filled with plush but empty pews. The podium at the end of the carpeted aisle beckoned me to advance to the front. Soon I would be preaching to 200 strangers, each with a need, a joy, and an unknown perspective on missions. Many Christians are overtly hostile to the missionary cause, I have discovered over the years. I found that I cannot exegete a congregation by gazing at the pews, and the pews finally stared me down. The alarm clock on the pulpit informed me that very few minutes remained.

Abruptly, visions of a packed-out church in Africa burst into my mind's eye. The pews were replaced with logs, the organ with a drum. My ears heard not the sedate and sensuous singing of hymns from the hymnal, but a standing, singing congregation chanting lyrics after their leader. The air was filled with smells of manioc and closely packed bodies. An occasional breeze served as the air conditioning.

Feelings of a complete inability to communicate anything to this community of Christians overwhelmed me. With a hard knot in my stomach I wondered if now I was a man without a culture. I looked at America through African eyes, and in spite of myself I looked at Africa through American eyes. Emotionally I am no longer a citizen of either country. My passport says American; my blood courses with African parasites. I am unsure to which tree my soul is grafted.

I walked down the side aisle to the narthex again. Still the church echoed only my sounds. I was estranged here because no links had been forged. Nothing had yet happened to tie me to this "supporting" church, nor this church to me. Shared experiences that create bonding belonged still to the future. I longed for one friend by whom I could stand for instant identification. I wished for a friend who would let me tag along.

The knee-level water fountain bent me into an inverted U as I attempted to get a drink. I turned the knob a little. No results. I turned it harder and was rewarded with a jet stream of water full in the face.

"Hello," rang a voice just behind me.

I straightened up, guiltily for some reason, wiping my dripping face with my suit sleeve. The water did not shut off and continued to arch over the fountain onto the floor. I kicked the fountain with my foot and the water receded.

"Hello," I replied. Then, dipping into my repertoire of polite dialogue, I added, "How are you?"

"Fine," he said, to no great surprise. He looked around. "Could you tell me where the bathroom is?"

A visitor! Like me!

"Over there. The light is behind the door when you go in," I replied knowingly. "Here, take a bulletin." I offered him one.

People began to arrive, and I began to stand around conspicuously. I played the game, "Who is the pastor?" and a variation on it, "Is there a missions committee chairperson?" Some people shook my hand and went by. My will to forcibly introduce myself had evaporated during my pulpit reverie of self-pity. I could not bring my mouth to say, "Hi, by the way, I'm your special guest missionary speaker. It is missionary emphasis Sunday, you know, I'm Brad, not Bard; from Africa, not China." So I waited, hoping to be recognized, and so valued. Silly, wasn't it?

"New here?" inquired someone. "Thought so," he said at my pre-oral nod, "Where you from?"

"Africa."

"Great, great. Good to have you here!" He shook my hand heartily. "Been going here myself for twenty years."

"Really? Say, that's quite a literature rack you've got here," I ventured.

He looked at me quizzically and went on to greet other arrivals. So did I.

Finally the pastor swished out of his office. His robe gave him away. He had, in forgivable ignorance, shaken my hand when he came in earlier.

"Where's that missionary?" he exclaimed, looking at his watch.

"Ready or not?" I said, by way of introduction.

He laughed out loud—a real unfeigned belly laugh. I warmed to him immediately. "I'm ashamed, really I am. But you shaved your beard! That picture on the bulletin board is an old one!" He was right. The pains of self-enforced anonymity began to fade.

We walked in together down the center aisle. A few people smiled in embarrassed recognition. I will admit to a perverse delight in their moment of realization, like the joke was on them.

The service was good. I was introduced right after "Bringing in the Sheaves" and "Rescue the Perishing." I stood to begin my sermon. All was going well, probably because I had given that sermon ten times before. I could have given it in my sleep; in fact I had.

I was just driving home point number ten (of twelve, for the tribes of Israel) when the alarm clock went off. I laughed and tried to speak louder, hoping its din would die. It just kept on jangling. I grappled with the clock and tried to strangle it, but I knocked it off the pulpit onto the floor where it continued undaunted. The congregation started to unravel. I stepped forward to retrieve the clanging Little Ben and kicked it with my foot over to the piano instead. Finally it gasped and deceased. I picked up the dead Ben and walked back over to the pulpit. At last the laughter died down to a twitter here and there.

"Now that I have your attention," I said, "I've lost my place and will have to start over."

Twitters became a collective groan. "Somebody play him back the end of the tape quickly!" shouted the pastor.

"Whatever happened to Bard?" came a voice.

"April fool!" The joke was on me.

Years later I look back at this as the beginning of a fine relationship with that church. We could laugh at each other, banter, and quip. The alarm was an embarrassment to us all, but it was the first shared experience. It plowed a passage through the ice. My feelings of desertion and non-identity were largely self-created, I realized. A new picture would have helped. Just a touch of initiative in introducing myself would have brought me immediately into the sphere of caring. I need not have played the neutral, dispassionate observer of life, floating in free space without that life-sustaining umbilical cord.

Prayerful and sacrificial sustenance undergirding our work now flows out from this church like a river glorious. They help make today worthwhile and enable us to face tomorrow. It was difficult to say au revoir at the airport, but the pain of separation in some way pointed ahead to the gain of mutual participation.

Four years later I returned to the church during furlough. The literature rack had not changed and the pictures were the same. But this time I was no stranger.

TWO
ROOTED

Our conversation while standing in front of the baggage counter is cheerful and upbeat. Ruth and I shove the carefully weighted suitcases a notch closer to the counter and a notch closer to departure. We talk about luggage allowances and air travel. Our parents stand near us, carrying the grandchildren, these same children who arrived in America a year ago speaking a Bantu dialect better than English. Now they have erased this Bantu Berlitz tape and speak only English. Grandma wears dark glasses to hide those wet blue-green eyes. The group of family and friends moves on toward the waiting area.

Jetting back and forth across the Atlantic to work is like thawing out a frozen fish, then freezing it again and again. Sooner or later the meat falls apart. We freeze our images of home: nephews who are young children, doting grandparents, youthful parents. Friends are still up and coming. We return to the States years later and thaw them out again, only to find that our images do not hold up. Cousins are barely recognizable, grandfather died, our parents have retired. Friends have now "made it." The sixteen-millimeter film of life is put on hold, then three years later is jumped ahead to the present.

A girl slides up to Ruth and slips her arm through hers. "Thanks for everything," she whispers. "I'll be praying for you." Ruth had walked with her through an unwanted pregnancy. They hug each other close.

"Brad, I'll mail you the project paper." This from one of my Sunday school students. Fresh from seminary myself, I had assigned a term paper on hermeneutics. She had come alive in this class, begun to ask questions and stretch, to break out her best.

I sit down with a group of friends I have grown up with. We suffered through confirmation together in junior high and wrote each other's letters home at summer camp. We ran track together in high school. The years apart saw us grow apart, and we do not seem to have very much to say. One member of the group is missing. He committed suicide.

Our family put down roots during this brief year home from the field. The tendrils of friendship had wound their way through the church's moist earth to join those of others. The Hill family thrived and bloomed. No, this 10:35 transplant to Africa would not be easy. Our souls would have to be grafted again into strange earth. Like Naaman, I wished to take it with me.

Under the canopy of arrival and departure announcements, we continue the rite of passage, each drawing from another assurances of continued love. We huddle around the fire of our human warmth, listening to the howling jet wind just outside. A jumbo jet skims down the runway building speed, and the conversation momentarily lapses. It is a harbinger of things to come. Dad jumps up to check the television monitor for the seventh time. The hour approaches; there will be no delay, no reprieve.

"Flight 627 is now ready for boarding." Families and handicapped would be boarding first.

Grandma tries to hand Becca back to Ruth. "You've got to go now, Becca." She clings tighter to her neck. Ruth pulls her gently but firmly, trying not to break the flower at the stem. Becca sobs, "I want Grandma."

Grandpa pulls us all together in a prayer circle. Arms on shoulders, we bow in the busy terminal to receive a blessing. People push past us; others stare in incomprehension, like they might at some unfathomable Hari Krishna rite. One or two smile in recognition of what we are about. This moment, too, is preserved on the mind's film. I record these last images of heads bowed, handkerchiefs out—last impressions to fill memory's scrapbook.

"Here, take this." Dad slips a bill into my hand.

We walk the gangplank down the ramp to the corner, then turn to wave back up the long inverted telescope at the little faces peering at us from the end. The flight attendant shows us to our seats; Rachel and I on the window side, Ruth and Rebecca across the aisle. Rachel opens and shuts the window cover to identify our seat.

"How long is three years, Daddy?"

Long enough to set down new roots, too short to forget. Rebecca will be twice as old when we return.

The plane crouches at the end of the runway, then starts its spring for the long transatlantic jump, hitting the takeoff in perfect stride. Ruth reaches across the aisle to find my hand. Seattle disappears under the heavy gray clouds, but soon we soar into a bright new day.

THREE
ON A WING AND A PRAYER
Excerpts from Our Travel Diary

T here was the inevitable snarl when I told the dour man in charge of the friendly skies that we wanted to check these bags through to Kolmejinahagba.

"You can't do that. You have to check them through to Paris, then to Kolwhatsamaface."

"Some people did it just last week," I replied. "Here's a copy of their baggage ticket." I shoved it across the counter at his winged chest.

He held it by one corner and examined it.

"Here's the call letters of the Kolmejinhagba airport." I handed him the slip of paper.

"Here's a letter from the airport manager saying we can do it." I handed it to him like passing a baton.

"The airport manager? O.K, O.K., fine with me, if it's fine with him." He surrendered under the artillery fire. You have to come prepared to these provincial air terminals, like O'Hare, that only know about routes to Moscow, Kiev, or Rio.

But I had to break his will, too. I fired the big one.

"Look at the computer screen. What do you see at the bottom?"

"Why, Mr. Hill, the manager actually punched it into the computer. . . ."

"We'll be on our way then. Gate 15?"

Our entire church, including backsliders, was waiting for us at the gate. "You shouldn't have," lied Ruth, with joy in her face. "Aren't these the best friends?" she said to anyone interested in the information. We said goodbye through runny mascara and survived charismatic-type hugs with only minor contusions.

Flight 007 took us to Paris. From there we took the train to Poupard, named after a famous mustard. Rachel was most fascinated with flushing the toilet onto the train tracks. She had to go every fifteen minutes.

Ever aware of her environment, she quickly fastened on the *Defense de Cracher* sign that was screwed in the wall just above the *Defense de Fumer* sign.

"Daddy, what does *Defense de Cracher* mean?" she asked when I read it to her.

"It means don't spit."

"I wasn't going to spit. Don't spit anywhere? Can't I spit outside?"

"Just not on the train." Rachel is like a scientist for whom a bit of information engenders more questions.

She looked all around. "I don't see anybody spitting."

"That's enough, Rachel."

"Do French people spit a lot?"

"No, I don't think they spit more than ordinary Americans."

The train pulled into Poupard and we took a taxi to an antiquated hotel near the center of town. Mom, my travel agent, had called ahead for reservations. Ruth and the girls disappeared through the door while I practiced my French on the unsuspecting taxi driver. I missed the price he mumbled through his Gallois cigarette. I leaned over to read the meter, but he anticipated me and punched the reset button.

"Here's septante franc," I finally said, thinking that was about right.

"Septante?" he snorted. "Where did you learn French? In Belgium?" he added in gleeful English.

"I didn't learn it in Dusseldorf," I shot back in quick repartee.

I went into the hotel looking for my family. They had evidently already gone up to the room. The proprietor caught the gist of my question and said, "Room 666 on the 13th floor." That made sense. I looked around the lobby. All I saw was a wooden staircase spiraling out of sight. Thirteen floors indeed! A little elevator was tucked under the corner of the *première etagé.* The door opened while I was trying to decipher the directions. A woman stepped out, and I stepped in. A look of consternation passed over her face. I could see her explaining something to me, with typical French reserve, through the little window. I gestured back with palms up.

The lift rose with a knee buckling lurch, the woman still signing. It slowed to a stop, but nothing happened. When I saw the handle and gave it a pull, the doors slid back into the wall and I stepped out into, well, the ladies' parlor. Needless to say, I did not do the American image abroad any favors standing there clutching Rachel's giant doll in the ladies' parlor. Fortunately there were only three or four women present. My Belgian French once again was not up to their remarks as I made for the exit.

Point No Point was an economy airline specializing in no frills—like windows. We were warned to come with coins for the pay toilets. "Limited overhead" meant no overhead luggage compartments. Their slogan was, "Pay now, fly if you dare." Undaunted, we called them on the *appareil.*

"Allo, allo?"

"Is this Point No Point Airlines?" I asked in French, though I should have known better.

"Allo, allo? *Qui est là?*"

"Yes, oui, is this Point No Point?"

"Yeah, what do you want?" came back the reply in American slang.

"Oui, er, yes, we're scheduled to leave for Kolmejinahagba tomorrow on flight #13. Could you confirm that?"

"Confirm it? Just a minute." He put his hand over the mouthpiece. "Jean, is there a flight out tomorrow?"

"Lemesee, here; just a minute. I don't think so. Oh, oui, I got it right here. I'll be darned, they are gonna fly tomorrow. They never tell me anything."

"Yes sir," came a crisp reply. "Just be here a little early."

"What's a little early?"

"About 4:00 a.m."

"For a 10:30 a.m. flight?"

"That's right, to avoid confusion." How can one help but be confused at four in the morning?

So we arrived at the crack of dawn in grey Poupard's airport. My family circled up the wagons defensively near the bathrooms and within field goal distance of the water fountain. I wandered down the floor looking for Point No Point's counter. There was none. Finally, in rising terror, I stopped a man with a mop.

"Point No Point?" He screwed up his face. Then the light dawned. "Oh yes, sure, they're here. The airport doesn't let them have a terminal of their own. Come with me."

He put his arm around my shoulder, perhaps to comfort me but also to guide me to the window.

"Look out there." He pointed between two planes, one a TWA and the other a KLM. Off in the distance was yet another 707. "I think that's it. Are you really flying with them, Monsieur?"

"Maybe not."

He shook my hand firmly. "Good luck."

I walked down to the Air Zimbabwe counter and surveyed the scene with cool aplomb. A gorgeous woman walked by, turning my head against my will. She had on a badge that said Point No Point pinned, well, just under the collar bone. I suppose I had unconsciously noticed the badge. That's why I looked.

"Excusez-moi, Madame," I stammered. "We're scheduled to leave on Point No Point for Kilomanjaro, I mean Komeini, Koldafy. . . ."

"Kolmejinahagba," she said.

"Oui, oui." The French never say "oui" just once. "Where's the counter?"

"I'm the counter, Monsieur." She flashed a smile at me. I sucked in my stomach. "Just give me your tickets."

I handed them over. "I should have bought them over the counter."

"Pardon, Monsieur?"

"Never mind." She punched the ticket and gave it back.

"Ah, er, excuse me again; seat number?"

"How do you say it—first come, first serve?"

That is how we say it, all right.

"Baggage check-in?"

"Just take it out to the airplane and load it there."

At 12:30 p.m. sharp we walked out across the tarmac. I pulled the Samsonite suitcase by the little strap, but the wheels had rusted and would not turn. Carrying it and Rebecca's three-foot "dolly," along with my Pentax zoom lens, made the going tough. We straggled into the airplane. Nobody checked our tickets; they would be glad to take anyone. You do not just wander out to this airplane by accident. They had checked us with a metal detector to see if we were adequately armed. The plane was only half full, but four seats together could not be found.

"Excusez-moi," I said to a defenseless looking little man with glasses. "Would you mind 'terriblement' if we sat together?" Ruth looked forlorn.

"Non, non, not at all; sit right down here, next to me."

"Non, non, not together with you; our family together, you know, four seats. . . ."

"No problem," he said, jumping over one seat. Now we had three in a row.

"I hate to bother you again, Monsieur, but could you move over one more seat?" He did not reply; he just slid over one.

Point No Point had fitted a dozen extra seats into the craft, putting my legs up into my chest. If the guy in front decided to lean back, they would have to disembark me with a crowbar. But I needn't have worried, for none of the seats tipped back.

"Ladies and gentlemen," came the announcement, "this is the captain speaking."

We waited expectantly for the rest of the announcement. That was it, but I had not taken exegesis for nothing. That phrase yielded a mine of information. We knew that the captain was present, that the P.A. worked (if the string to the tin can did not break), and that some ladies and gentlemen were assumed present.

We were given clearance, and the jet waddled out to the end of the strip. The Fasten Your Seat Belt sign went off just as we surged forward. The captain put the Boeing into a sharp turn so we could take one last longing look at downtown Poupard.

About nightfall, I began to notice a little moisture filtering down from somewhere. The sky outside was clear; besides, airplanes don't leak rain, do they? The flight attendant was not to be seen. The mist turned into droplets, increasing in volume. I pulled the flight attendant button and my seat went back. I finally caught her eye by putting up my umbrella. The man behind me began to laugh, but just then the air conditioning spewed out about a liter of ice water into his lap. I excused his French.

The Toilet Occupied lights went on and off as people walked up to the front and returned to their seats. Rachel nudged me.

"Does the airplane flush into the sky like a bird?"

Point No Point held no more surprises for me. "Probably."

The seat-belt signs blinked on and the *Defense de Fumer* sign blinked off as we prepared to land somewhere. Rachel noticed it right away.

"Daddy, can I spit on the airplane?"

By all means, I thought.

PART TWO

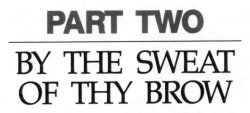

BY THE SWEAT
OF THY BROW

*Missionaries expect that somewhere, sometime,
the structure will balance with the theology.*

PERSPECTIVE

The true Church as a communion of people called out by God for a special purpose is not always discernible in the local congregation. African churches are no exception. The Holy Spirit's creation of a body of saints living on principles of justice, love, and equality seems academic amid the missionary's work of balancing budgets, cleaning kitchens, killing cockroaches, and arbitrating disputes. The structure of our work chokes the very breath of life that transported us to a new continent in the first place.

My French-English dictionary tells me that a *bilan* is a balance sheet or evaluation. Missionaries expect that somewhere, sometime, the structure will balance with the theology. But in making a *bilan,* we experience a dose of disillusionment. We expect a measure of gratitude from villagers and church leaders blessed with our presence. Often we are told that we have failed because of our short-sightedness and that the national church is groping its way in and out of ditches because missionaries are afflicted with glaucoma—if not blindness.

The fault is not entirely with the structure. Perhaps it sounds platitudinous to say, "Put people first," but there it is. My own *bilan* shows that I have invested too much time in machinery to the detriment of people. I have built buildings that will someday squeak their hollow songs. I have written treatises that will crumble into dust. I have been too busy to deal with a personal problem, too occupied to exercise a pastoral role.

Such a *bilan* is sobering. The past is gone.

Such a *bilan* is renewing. The future beckons.

FOUR

THE CLAMOR OF VOICES

Slowly my mind swims for the surface of consciousness. It is a long way to go from the murky depths of contented REM. Several times the yawning deep beckons me back. Finally, I break the still surface of sleep, feeling like Jaws. Thinking, I float on the gentle surface swells, not yet ready to begin the day's sea hunt.

What stands out about the last few weeks is nothing. I have been very busy, but have accomplished nothing of importance. I have been getting plenty of exercise on a treadmill, finishing each day sweaty and exhausted without having gone anywhere. The mundane has straddled those weeks and dominated every aspect of existence. Where are the sweet days of spiritual expectancy and peering with baited breath around the corner of each day to see what God will bring? Perhaps missions are like some marriages I have known. The initial euphoric rapture fades into the commonplace, and the first blush of young love becomes an embarrassed memory. Ritual and roles map out the course of the marriage. Words are exchanged, but there is no communication. Have I lost my first love? Where is the voice of the Bridegroom?

I disentangle myself from the mosquito net, eager not to begin another day. Groping feebly for the flashlight and not finding it, I stagger into the kitchen and light the gas stove by touch. By the light of the soft blue flame I manage to light a lamp and wait for the coffee water to boil. A glance at my watch tells me I have missed my devotion time again. I will have to hurry, regardless of spiritual bends.

The "ko ko ko" that serves as an oral doorbell interrupts my attempt to read the coffee grounds in the bottom of my plastic Winnie-the-Pooh mug. In three syllables our young yard worker has signaled his presence, his need for the cookhouse key, and his contempt for those who sleep in. I get up and give him the keys.

Ruth is now up and arrives in time to give instructions to our indispensable and cherished *domestique,* who had just punched in with his cheery "ko ko ko." As I try to ready myself for the exciting day, Ruth begins the long process of bartering rock salt for eggs that don't float and clothing for firewood.

My floating-head shaver didn't charge last night, and I stare balefully at it, undecided whether I should skip a day or use a twenty-five-cent Bic shaver. I don't have to use one, but I do.

On my way out the door to unlock the school, I grab a handful of keys —keys to the school, keys for the garage, keys to the woodshop, for the storeroom, the trucks, and the generator house. Along with the keys of the kingdom comes a large key ring. All the keys bulging in my pocket remind me again of the inexhaustible supply of trivia that I must shovel through. Sometimes as much time seems to be spent on mission maintenance as in spiritual conquest.

My day began formless and void, but now the winds blow and the agenda takes shape. Check with the carpenter on the cabinet, stop by the chauffeur's house because he is sick. Lay out the septic tank floor so that it is square, or plumb, or level, or something. Try to make my class in Revelation. Today's subject is the three dirty frogs.

Slowly the day grinds down like our hard-to-start truck. Soon after lunch my Die-Hard battery is just about dead. I settle down in my office to fill out the quarterly reports and pension sheets. When that is done, I can move on to planning next week's seminar on family planning.

Then, just as the first pregnant thought activates my pen, there is that faint but nevertheless psyche-shattering "ko ko ko." A man is sick and needs to be rushed to the hospital. Our driver is also under the weather, I remember. The seminar will have to wait. I sigh. Another workout on the treadmill looms ahead.

The truck catches on the fourth try, which is better than usual, and we head for the hospital. Now the tension of the time presses down on the accelerator. "If I hurry, I can return by four-forty and still get my work done as planned." But halfway from anywhere, which is really nowhere, the truck coughs, sputters, and jerks to an abrupt halt, along with all my family planning. The seminar will certainly be delivered late now. I bang both hands on the wheel in frustration.

At first I just feel irritated and grind the battery down to nothing in a futile effort. Then I check under the hood. Mustering my considerable mechanical skill, I size up the motor and decide it is all there. I wiggle the air filter; it is on tight. The groans of the sick man break through the reverie of self-pity.

Then the still small voice of the Lord whispers. At first I am not sure what it is. I am the opposite of Paul's traveling companions—I hear the voice but do not see any light. He speaks again, slowly for my benefit.

"For whom are you concerned?"

I know the answer to that one: me, not the sick man.

"Slow down. My time is your time, my plans are yours. Rest in me and recover your peace. Wait upon me and pray. I have given you more than enough time in this day that I have created to do what I want you to do."

I shut the hood and begin to pray silently.

"Not silently, out loud. You know what to pray for."

"Out loud? But what if it doesn't start? I probably need to bleed the lines before I pray, don't you think. . . ?"

No answer. Reluctantly, I have all the passengers bow in prayer, and feeling not a trifle vulnerable I ask the Lord to start the truck and get this man to the hospital. I get in the truck already thinking of theologically laden explanations to give my passengers as to why it did not start. I put my hand on the key, and with eyes tightly shut, turn it. "You're the one with his neck on the block, Lord," I cajole.

It starts, dead battery and all. I shift into gear and head for the hospital. Somebody behind me offers the thanks I forgot in my amazement.

FIVE

CHICKEN LITTLE

Two thousand singing, straining, sweating, swaying people packed the church as tightly as a grease gun. I sat in front in the little pocket of air reserved for honored guests. My heart soared on song's wings, and my body—at first reluctantly, then with increasing abandon—succumbed to the pulsating reverberations of the brass drum. And I wondered what that little chicken was doing behind the podium.

The evangelism team had been in the area for a week. Every evening the people came and kept coming. The revival fires were strong; no sinner was left unscorched. Hundreds had came forward to renew publicly their commitment to the Lord.

The team occasionally invited a missionary to go along, but it was headed by the church's national evangelist. The large building in which we gathered had burnt to the ground only two months before, and I marveled at the industry that rebuilt it so quickly. I reflected that no conference at home could boast eighty churches and 24,000 members. This region had, under excellent leadership, pushed ahead with programs of fishponds and sawmills. Giving was up, and they were able to buy their superintendent a new Kawasaki. I was pleased to be there and was poised on the brink of preaching one of the sermons of my life on the filling of the Holy Spirit, who gives power to his Church for holiness and ministry.

The superintendent stood to introduce the morning speaker—me. I smiled with modest expectancy, ready to rise and unsheath the sword of the Spirit. He motioned for me to stand up, then he reached down and grabbed the little chicken by its bound feet. It fluttered and squawked, then quieted down.

"This scrawny little chicken," he began addressing the church, "represents the church that the missionaries bequeathed us." Then he turned to me. "You came with a gospel of heaven and hell, but left out earth;

and so this church remains thin, poor, underdeveloped, and sick.''

My ears roared with blood, and I missed the next few sentences. I was a sitting duck in front of the chicken. Inwardly I reeled at the force of these accusations. I took them personally. I was one with the mission, however much I might wish to disassociate myself from past mistakes. Chagrin turned to anger. These accusations were twisted half-truths, veiled slander, launched at an inappropriate moment.

''. . . Forgot the body, forgot to teach us your secrets of gaining wealth. Why should the servants of the Lord, he who has the cattle on a thousand hills, have to walk? Why should their children not go to the universities? How shall we white-haired pastors live in our old age? We have nothing. You missionaries have maybe helped some, but really, not very much.''

I could not maintain one consistent emotion. My resentment boiled over. After fifty years and a church of 85,000 members, should I accept the shame shoveled on me by this description of need? What mission organization would be capable of making their daughter churches wealthy and independent of local economy? Or would even want to?

The superintendent held up the chicken for all to see, then offered it to me. My hands went up to take it in spite of my resolution to leave them by my side.

''Just as this feeble chicken is in your hands to do with as you please, so the church is in your hands. You can kill it now and eat its mouthful, or you can grow it, develop it, so that it becomes big and strong. It's up to you.''

By now my eyes were a brimming cauldron of tears, and finely blended feelings of shame-outrage and anger-sorrow tore at me. I yearned to wring the chicken's scrawny neck then and there, but no, that was too brutal. I would simply hand it back with the comment, ''No, its your scrawny chicken, not mine''—a fine gesture of self-absolution. But as usual I was too polite and culturally sensitive (read: chicken) to do anything other than stand there in numb compliance.

The cruel little ceremony concluded and he turned back to the unusually quiet congregation.

''The missionary with the chicken will come now and open God's Word to us. Come!'' He beckoned to me.

I laid the little chicken by my chair and walked to the podium. A long, deep inhalation preceded a rather antiseptic ''Hello.'' The answering ''Hello'' was also subdued. The room was charged, alive with anticipation and anxiety. How would this missionary respond? The superintendent had taken a dreadful chance in turning over the pulpit to me. In fact it showed his faith in me to do so.

I decided to absorb the ignominy like a paper towel. As I stood to preach, it dawned on me how the very fact that I was invited to preach after such an introduction was missions in microcosm. We were castigated but trusted; criticized but then given the pulpit; blamed but then believed.

I was in effect being invited to preach the shalom of the whole Gospel. Perhaps the sky had not fallen on my head after all, but rather heaven had come down and glory could fill our souls.

The chicken squawked loudly at my feet as if to tell me he was not as feeble as everyone imagined.

SIX

OF MACHINES AND MEN

Ona of the church regions was about to split like a ripe mango over tribal issues. The unity of the body was in jeopardy. The regional leaders had called for help, and several of us pastors came in response to their SOS. But once there, our advice had been rejected, and we ourselves had come under fire.

I was disgusted with the church. As I walked along the path leading away from it, I was not going anywhere; it was just essential that the path go away from the ugly scene. It was a riot of shouting, angry Christians, with name-calling and insinuation. A grenade burst of long stored-up grievances spewed the shrapnel of hate throughout the assembly. When the energies were spent and each side carted off its wounded and dead to lick their wounds and eat lunch, I took off. What was the use of investing in a church like that? The issues were many: a couple of preachers had taken second wives; another had been called a "Togbo" (how would you like to be called a Togbo?), a slanderous name derived from a former slave tribe; the treasurer had stolen some funds; the superintendent did not care about their needs, and they wanted to become independent. When I attempted to voice my opinion, it was made clear that my opinion carried about as much weight as a helium balloon. Fine. I wouldn't give it anymore. I would pout. And if what I said to the people was not wanted, neither was what I did for them. Why knock myself out in the Bible school producing preachers like that? Why build buildings, grow coffee, or even make evangelism trips if this was their gratitude? People! Fie!

I suddenly found myself before a nice brick house. I was amazed. In the middle of the jungle? A man came out and greeted me.

"I'm the caretaker of this plantation," he said proudly, sweeping his hand and imaginatively taking in the "plantation." I've got a loony, I thought. All I could see around me was dense underbrush.

"Yes," he said, noting my lack of wonder. "This used to be a plantation of 100-square kilometers of rubber, coffee, rice, palm trees, fishponds,
cattle. Like a tour Mister?"

Feeling a little like Alice in Wonderland, I agreed. As we walked, he
gestured expansively to the right and majestically to the left, telling me
with great vigor what used to be there. With some mind-expanding mental
gymnastics I vaguely visualized rows of palm trees; indeed many still
stood, unkempt. As he described the enormous fruit harvest of the long-
past Death Valley Days, a group of juvenile thieves whipped past us with
handfuls of stolen oranges—this year's entire crop. We followed the cur-
vature of a large fishpond that could have raised small whales. Then we
came to the work camp.

The work camp? I could hear twenty-mule-team Borax in the back-
ground. Perhaps fifty houses stood in a row. Each small adobe house
was precariously perched atop a yard of eroded foundation. They reminded me of embarrassed pelicans caught washing. Children were playing
while men and women sat in front of the houses and watched us pass.

"What, er, do they do, you know, for work?"

"Nothing."

"I see," I lied.

Here was a ghost plantation with non-existent crops, inhabited by
unemployed workers.

"Look, over there, do you see the boss's house?"

It could only have been the boss's house. Seemingly it was modeled
after Versailles and the Grande Place combined. Sightless windows stared
silently back; broken doors squeaked their ancient song of emptiness.

Next on the itinerary was the office. The structure still stood. It was
all there, but nothing was there. I moved about the spacious quarters raising clouds of dust. On a shelf I brushed off a folder that read "Rubber
Production Figures for 1949." I opened another and pulled a page yellow
and brittle with age. I read, "Fish Culture in the Belgian Congo." I ginger-
ly replaced it. Adjacent to the office were huge storerooms. The caretaker
opened one, and we stepped into the cavernous crypt. Several sacks of
long-since rotted rice were piled in a corner. Rats scurried around seek-
ing refuge. In the center of the floor stood a rice winnower that looked
oiled and in good shape. I stared. It was like finding a golden transistor
in King Tut's tomb.

Noting my wonder, the caretaker said, "I oil it often."

"For what?"

He stared at me uncomprehendingly.

It was too much. I did not dare ask why, with what oil, or for how
long, for fear that the Twilight Zone answers would seize me and bundle me across the threshold.

I started back to the church. The next round would soon begin, each
side having gathered its parliamentarian heavyweights. But at least the
issues here were of flesh and Spirit, and not oil and empty ponds.

Upon my return, I expected to reenter the fray, but as I walked into the mud and thatch church I was amazed to see several men grouped in a circle, holding hands, voices raised to God in prayer. The Spirit of God had descended between rounds.

No hollow, dusty footfalls of an irreverent stranger will ring through an empty church, and no one will write the church's obituary with, ''My what beautiful buildings. What do they mean?''

PART THREE
MIRTH IN OUR TEARS

*Culture shock is the anxiety that results from
losing all your familiar signs.*

PERSPECTIVE

We are inextricably bonded to our own culture. Social intercourse is a matter of instinct and reflex action. We are at ease and comfortable. But what happens when, with the price of a one-way ticket and in a matter of hours, you are wrenched from television, Big Macs, and English and thrown into a milieu of drums, manioc root, and "gibberish"?

Suddenly even knowing how to greet a person becomes a chore. Nobody laughs at your jokes, or they laugh and you do not. They wash your water glass in the dirty hand basin. Nobody hurries when you are pressed, but suddenly everything happens without warning. You do not have a dog or a cat for a pet; you have a monkey, an anteater, or a parrot. Your servant gossips in the village about your sex life, and the children harvest all your oranges, grapefruits, papayas, pineapples, guavas, and avocados. And palm nuts. Mice seem to thrive on your poison, and you cannot believe it is good to have gecko lizards on your screens.

Culture shock is the anxiety that results from losing all your familiar signs. The missionary arrives as a tourist; it is fun, exciting, and the camera whirrs. But sooner or later you realize that this is not just a long layover. This realization produces a syndrome of rejection, either of the host country or your own. Complaining and fault-finding permeate everything. Feelings of failure and guilt are common; one may reject even God.

By the grace of God and ample patience all around, the missionary passes on to the third stage and becomes a humorist. This is not laughing at the culture; rather, it is perceiving and even enjoying the dissonance and incongruities that plague life. You are able to joke about your own shortcomings and blunders.

This humor also punctuates the fourth stage—adjustment. The missionary achieves a new economy of living. In spite of times of strain and stress, the missionary sees the culture as essentially valid and adaptive for the people. Eagerness for discovery and learning characterize the missionary's life.

Home becomes an ambiguous word.

SEVEN
THE TIRED DOGS OF WAR

Gbamajonga, I had heard, was a three-hour walk through elephant grass. That did not sound too difficult for one who kept in shape by running five miles a day. But one can never be sure about African distances. I thought, ah, yes, Gbamajonga, another remote village reached and explored by that intrepid missionary adventurer, Brad Hill. Today, the name Gbamajonga can still bring nightmares.

We arrived late at the trail's head, and the porters had already left. I hoisted the twenty-five-pound pack on my back, and a kind woman took my water jug. After the first hour in the searing heat, we crossed a river. Soon we crossed another. And a third. We continued to forge ahead. No shade under the trees, for we were in *sobi*, or elephant grass, and it had been recently burned. Blisters began to form on my feet from the wet and dirt. That was but the beginning of woes.

My water had raced on ahead of us on the woman's head and was not to be seen again. My sunglasses had fallen off somewhere, and I began to suffer from glare. Blisters began to break open about five hours along. A splitting headache began its touchdown drive in the cerebellum, made quick yardage across the corpus callosum, and scored in the cerebrum. The extra point was kicked into my optic nerve.

Soon the sun set and prompted another discovery: my flashlight did not work.

I stumbled into Gbamajonga with the rising moon and collapsed into a chair. I was feverish, and the night air made me feel I was on Mt. Rainier. For an hour I did not move. I just twitched. Then grudgingly I went inside to eat a meal of manioc and dried fish.

Even though the small wicker bed in the warm hut seemed divine, sleep eluded me. The headache, chills and sweats, and the hard bed made that an impossible dream. The next day the ache was worse, much worse. Even going to the *Yoane* (that's "john" in dialect) was excruciating. I did not move from the chair all day.

The next night was no better. The niviquine seemed to help the fever, but a sick child cried all night long right next to me. As Sunday dawned, I wondered how on earth I was going to preach the heavenly message. But as time marched on, somehow in a haze and daze of misery, I preached the message and the service was over. I looked down at my hand being pumped and realized that somebody was saying, "Nice service, Reverend." I wondered what I had said.

Finally, about noon, with the sun again overhead, we made preparations to return. My headache was quite a bit better, but the fever lingered on. The major problem was the open blisters. I just hobbled on the sides of my feet the best I could. My mind rebelled at the skull-and-crossbones reality that lay ahead; surely I did not really have to make the eight-hour trek back to the truck, crippled, feverish, and weak from too little food and sleep! There had to be a better idea, a short cut, some magic . . . a miracle?

The water got ahead of me again, so I did not get any for the first two hours. We had all regrouped at the first river crossing. As I tipped the jug back and let the cool water course down my throat, I shut my eyes. I didn't want to see my thirsty traveling companions staring at me. I tried to summon up all my latent selfishness and keep the jug to myself, but I failed. I watched in helpless horror as it was passed around. An hour later it was all gone.

We trudged on. The open blisters screamed expletives at me when I crossed the river barefoot. It seemed like salt water; it was just the sand.

I resorted to head games: don't look at the watch until you're sure it's past a certain time; then look and be surprised how long you've gone! Count to a thousand then look at the watch. Repeat songs and verses, look at the watch. Pray, and don't look at the watch. The only thing that kept me going was the vision of Ruth welcoming me, pulling off my shoes and bloody socks, handing me a tall cool one, and generally pampering me.

We stopped for a break at about the halfway point. No way was I going to make it another four hours in that *sobi*. I pictured them carrying me out on a stretcher. For the first time I began to wonder if there was supposed to be some redeeming value to this experience, i.e., a lesson. Neither my brain nor my spirit was working well enough to find one.

Time moved along with all the zest of a slug crossing the Utah salt flats. I entered a timeless state. I had to walk directly on the huge blisters because my feet were cramping up from walking on the sides. One river nearly swept me off my feet. After crossing another—the last—I laid down and stretched out immobile for about ten minutes. Finally, I swept aside the cobwebs as a timid hand was feeling for my heart. They thought I was dead! Like a newborn lamb I struggled to my feet and climbed the last hill, followed the ridge and descended to the village where the truck awaited our return.

Just as we had finished packing the Land Rover for our three-hour return trip, a man came and begged us to take his dying son to his village, forty-five minutes in the opposite direction. Once again I found my selfishness insufficient to overcome my pity. We loaded him in with all the mourners. He died en route. Upon arrival at his village, a quick wake was organized. It began to look like an all-night affair. However, being sure that if such were the case they would have to mourn my passing as well, I said I was leaving in thirty minutes and did. My riders scrambled to get in, and we headed for home. The whole ride was a blur. I did not have enough strength to use the brakes, so I used the shock absorbers instead. A tropical downpour turned the muddy road into a fish ladder. I would have sold my soul for the end of the trip.

Ruth was there when I arrived. It was all over. I tried to cry, but dehydration and fatigue just turned the effort into dry sobs.

Two days after the trip, my blisters were peeled back and infected. I was getting antibiotic injections and missing school. The intrepid adventurer was no more. In fact, he had never been. I have no desire to live up to that image any longer. Just give me my comforts on the station, thank you. Just let me take my place among the rank and file.

EIGHT

THE MIDNIGHT RUN OF REVEREND HILL

In the Land Rover I had often bounced over the rugged twenty-five-mile stretch of road between the mission hospital and our little mission station hidden away in Africa's jungles. As the roads deteriorated during rainy season, so did my patience. Finally, after one particularly frustrating trip, I foolishly declared, "I can run it faster than I can drive it!" And thus began the saga.

I had been a serious fair-weather jogger for years, averaging fifteen to twenty miles a week. I figured, somehow, that if I could increase my mileage to fifty miles a week for two weeks, I could make it to the hospital. My wife agreed that that was exactly where I would end up.

As my mileage increased, I began to suffer from the tropical heat. At four in the afternoon with both humidity and temperature between eighty and ninety degrees, I felt as though I was running in a greenhouse. I stepped inside after one long run. My wife looked up and said, "Oh, did it rain? I didn't notice."

I switched to morning running. I had to be at the school by six so I began my run at four in the morning—in the dark. Sometimes it was exhilarating with the crystal-clear stars overhead; occasionally I would see a satellite or a comet. When the full moon was up, it breathtakingly illuminated the road and villages. Finally, I could run ten miles at an eight-minute pace. I felt I was ready.

But I needed to plan carefully. There would be no way stations, restrooms, ambulances, or other runners. No free T-shirts, but no entrance fees, either. The run would have to be in the morning so as to profit from the coolness. I would need three consecutive days without rain or the roads would be too muddy. A light-weight flashlight would be a must. But what about fluids? And a backup? I arranged for our mission's chauffeur to follow in the Land Rover (if it could keep up!). He would have lime Kool-Aid and could rush me to the hospital should I collapse. My wife told me just to go directly to the hospital and bypass "Go."

Finally, all fell into place. I got up at 2:45 a.m., ate a banana, and spent some time stretching. At 3:30 a.m. the chauffeur arrived, and I was off. It was a cool, moonless morning. A cloud cover made it as black as night, which of course it was. My bouncing little flashlight showed up the puddles all right, but my depth perception was off. I continually stumbled, slipped, and slid until daybreak. Knees and ankles took a beating. I was comforted to think the Land Rover was just out of sight behind me and the hospital was just ahead.

As I jogged along at daybreak, the birds began to cheer me on. Various jungle noises caught my attention, such as the crunching of a millipede underfoot. I was blissfully thinking myself in harmonious relationship with God's nature when there was a savage snort and a ferocious rustling of bushes not a yard from me. I reacted with a startled yell and a personal best in the quarter mile. I probably wasted thirty minutes of running energy.

At the halfway point, the truck pulled up alongside me. I tossed my flashlight inside and grabbed the bottle of lime Kool-Aid. One gulp told me that I should not have mixed it at 2:45 a.m. I must have quadrupled the sugar quota. The sticky, sweet liquid coated my mouth and throat, and no amount of expectoration would clear it.

Now all the villages were wide awake. As I entered a village, everyone would line up along the road and stare. Mothers would hide their little children behind them and point. A few would try to say hello, but mostly they just stared. Halfway through one village I heard footsteps behind me. I turned to see a couple dozen youngsters following me. I felt like the Pied Piper.

At about the eighteen-mile mark, I entered a series of exhausting hills. My chauffeur was getting worried about me, so he pulled up to within three yards of my flagging derrière. I tried to signal him to back off, but he just waved and maintained his protective distance. The first hill was a mile long and steep. I did not dare stop for fear of being rear-ended. The downhill made my knees feel like a slinky toy descending steps. The next hill, short and very steep, was nearly my obituary. I jerked and clawed the air to the top. The quizzical villagers watched this utterly fascinating spectacle in silent wonder. Finally one fellow expressed the collective mind by asking, "Where are you going?"

"To the hospital," I gasped.

"Thought so," he rejoined.

Further along another agog African ventured a hopeful, "What are you doing?"

I had plotted this answer for miles. "I'm pulling the truck!"

The chauffeur shook his head vigorously and shouted back, "No, I'm chasing him!"

Finally, the hills were behind me and only a couple of miles remained. My jello knees could not hold me any longer, and even VISA could not carry my oxygen debt. I decided to quit. Close enough. I signaled to the truck, and he pulled alongside. Maybe the devil made me do it, I don't know, but, aghast, I heard myself say, "Go wait at the end." And off he went, but not before his tire smashed into a large puddle covering me from trembling tip to tired toe with muddy water green with frog eggs.

Ten minutes later, after four hours of jogging, I pulled into the hospital compound. I could not decide whether to go first to the emergency ward or to the maternity ward, where they had the best beds and I could put my feet up. But just then our nurse came out. She took one look at me and exclaimed cleverly, "Whatever happened to you?"

Again, I had had ample time to come up with a memorable quote, but oxygen debt had already bankrupted my brain. I managed a sickly-sweet, lime-green smile and said, "Didn't you notice? It rained."

The Land Rover still holds the record.

NINE
SPIRIT WARS

Ithat would be my turn next. I was prepared to lie through my teeth. I would do the very thing I hate, yet the Spirit sets his desire against the flesh so that I cannot freely do the things I please.

That morning I had left the mission to do some business in town, an hour-and-a-half drive away. All business is transacted between eight-thirty and eleven-thirty. The anxious early bird is rewarded with the same absent worm as the late sloth, that is, with vacant offices. I had vowed to arrive at eight-thirty, and it was just past seven. My inner time clock went off like the alarm at the fire station. It was time to cut my losses and run. I moved quickly to the truck.

"Wait, I'll fix you a road lunch," Ruth said.

"No thanks, I'll just buy some cassava bread later," I replied with a martyr's smile. "Gotta go."

"But what about your passenger, Kolombo; you promised him a ride. He isn't here yet."

"Kolombo? This trip isn't for him; he's along for the free ride. He'll just have to find another way."

I hopped in and started the truck, crunching it quickly into reverse. "You didn't forget your driver's license again, did you?"

Why was Ruth trying to make me late? Furthermore, she did not have to remind me as if I were a forgetful little boy. I did not like the particular accent on "again," either. I could remember my license all by myself, most of the time. I felt my pocket; then the other pocket. I tried to focus an intimidating frown at her.

"I didn't forget it," I fibbed; "I just couldn't find it. Well," I added airily, "gotta go; no more time. Besides, the police never check trucks anymore." Where there is no law, there is no sin. That's Scripture, I mused. I started to back up, then stopped. Ruth was standing there with her arms crossed.

"Oh gosh, honey, I'm not that pressed. I certainly have time for a kiss."

That was guilt speaking. A quick kiss was all time allowed because Ruth doesn't like to kiss while I'm backing up the truck. I received one of those perfunctory pecks that makes you feel worse afterward. I glanced at my Seiko chronograph as I pulled out. 7:07:13.10.

Kolombo was on the road and he managed to jump in at ten miles per hour, gaining us thirty more seconds.

A few minutes later he spoke. "Pastor Hill, we haven't prayed yet."

"Yes, right. O.K. Dear Lord, help us to get there by eight-thirty. Amen." I did not hear an answering "Amen" from Kolombo.

We rode in silence as I expertly drove the truck into potholes and over baby chicks that lagged behind their mothers, crossing the road.

I slowed as we neared the city. Rounding a corner, I was forced to break to a halt behind a line of trucks. Since there are not enough vehicles to make a traffic jam, I reasoned that there must be an accident ahead. I strained to see. It was eight-twenty-five. Finally I was able to see what was causing the slow-up. A policeman wearing the distinctive white helmet and gloves was examining papers at a checkpoint. I felt like I had just swallowed a large ice cube. The only accident would soon be mine. He waved a truck on, and the line advanced.

I knew there was another little-used road into town, about a mile back. I started to back up to turn around as a big Mercedes truck filled my rear-view mirror. We moved up another notch. I tried to make a U-turn only to find that I had just moved up to the road divider. I was snared like an antelope swinging from a tree awaiting the hunter.

My whole life flashed before my eyes. The highlights of my childhood were all there. I remembered a cartoon of a certain lady mouse tied to a conveyor belt inexorably moving her towards a saw. Just as the saw began to cut her shoes, Mighty Mouse flew down and rescued her. I always tend to get theological at times like these. I glanced up at the sky.

I resolved to take my medicine, but only if I had to. I could tell the policeman that I was just on my way to the police station to get my license. I could look all over the cab with increasing desperation, then say it had fallen out . . . no, stolen, yes, stolen!

We moved up another notch. Only two trucks ahead of me.

I could stall the truck and walk into town to get a part. I could calmly hand him my Sears charge card—with a neatly folded bill behind it. I could curse all these drivers ahead of me who had their papers in order.

I was sweating, my heart pounding. Gastric acid poured mercilessly upon my linings.

One truck ahead.

I had one other alternative. It was unheard of and would never work. It was too implausible. I could tell the truth. I turned the phrase "I forget it" over in my mind a couple of times. I tried it in dialect, then French.

I rehearsed a scenario in which I smiled stupidly and said it in English.

The policeman was arguing with the driver of the truck in front of me. Something was not in order. I watched, fascinated. When my turn came, I would turn down the blindfold.

The least that could happen would be to pay a fine on the spot. The worst would be to go to the station and wait hours, fill out forms, and pay a big fine, then try to get the impounded vehicle back. As I watched the scene in front of me, I knew with certainty that my fate was sealed, judgment and sentence passed. I even knew that I deserved it.

When faced with inevitable punishment, I always dip into my accumulated reserve of guilt to make it pay. Yes, I merited a fine and worse. I had kissed Ruth in reverse. I had been ready to abandon my passenger for the sake of a few seconds. I had left my license deliberately—intentionally. I had broken the law with malice aforethought. Biblically, I was in the category of the "high-handed sinner" for whom there was no offering to be made. I had committed these crimes for an arbitrary deadline of eight-thirty that I myself had set. I was caught, guilty as Goldilocks.

The soldier walked around to the passenger side of the first truck and got in. It started up and, in a cloud of diesel exhaust, rolled up the road.

I looked around when the fumes blew off. No police in sight. I just sat there, stunned. What should I do? The road was clear but I was still guilty. Should I drive to the station and turn myself in? I had received a suspended sentence. My heartbeat diminished, but I still gripped the steering wheel with sweaty palms.

Kolombo looked at me oddly. "Why don't you go?" he asked reasonably.

Of course, all of the lies and scenarios had been enacted in my head. To him I was just waiting impatiently to go. Relief washed over me. I sighed deeply. I had been liberated, freed without price. The other driver had taken my place. I deserved to be hauled in, but I was now released, redeemed, forgiven, and given another chance.

The Mercedes behind me gave us a blast with his foghorn. I shifted into gear and went into town, only a few minutes late.

TEN
NIGHT CRAWLERS

Rustle, scrape, scurry, slither, squeak, creak, clunk, baa, snort: the night sounds begin to lull me to sleep. Within my mosquito net tucked in snugly around my blanket, I lay my head back on my wadded jeans, trying to find, futilely of course, a more comfortable position on the hard reed bed. And I wait. It will start soon, the nighttime lullaby of the jungle concerto. How many nights does this make, serenaded to sleep by these sounds? How many times over these last years have I been startled to instant wakefulness by them?

It begins with the faint whine of mosquitoes, no doubt a family that claims the hut for themselves. They come nearer, and I hear them surrounding the net to cut off my escape. They test my mesh, my defense perimeter, probing for holes. Some are inches away from my ear, but as time passes and none get past my Star Wars defense, my body slowly relaxes and waits for the second movement.

There is a rustle of leaves over my head. I identify it as a mouse and trace its path across the thatch, until with a thump and a bump, his allegro ends. Peace of mind comes from quick identification of the various pieces. There is nothing that ruins my sleep more thoroughly than a UJS— Unidentified Jungle Sound, like wondering if what I hear over my head is a mouse or a mamba, a poisonous snake.

Now in quick succession come the slithering sounds of a lizard, the faint disturbances of an inch-long cockroach exploring my dinner table, and the squeak and the creak that signal my neighbor's restless sleep in the adjacent room.

My mind just begins to wander into vague dreams when a snort brings all my senses to acute focus. A snort? In my room? Desperately I grope for my flashlight, find it, and push the button. Nothing. There it is again, several different snorts in fact. Frantically I shake and bang the Shanghai-made flashlight, and it produces a faint flickering glow. I sweep the room; there is nothing. But, there, I hear it again. It is outside. Goats. The goats are settling in for the night just on the other side of my porous wall. I push the button to off, and the light brightens up. A bang and a shake with reverse english kills the light. I fluff up my Sears Tall-Man jeans and lie back.

The mouse begins industriously gnawing away at something. I listen carefully; he is gnawing on wood. Nothing of mine. A couple of small squeaks signal the arrival of wife and children.

Again the line between reality and dream begins to blur. An image of Room 722 of the Hyatt Regency in Phoenix floats by, and I grab for it as an official dream. Phoenix, Covenant, Annual Meeting . . . ordination. . . .

Another unidentifiable noise. What is it? A flurry of, yes, feathers. Feathers . . . cluck, nonthreatening noises. I recall the hole under the door and surmise that the mother hen and chicks just made their entrance. I decide against another attempt to master Chinese technology.

A faint tickle under the covers stiffens my body. Now, will it move? Or is it just a sweat-plastered hair springing up? I wait, the tickle moves. Again the performance is repeated with the flashlight. It comes on, attracting little gnats through the net and onto the glass. I peer curiously under the blanket and see nothing. But, there it is, just a small nondescript bug, which dies an indescribable death.

Now the sounds of silence dominate. I grope again for 722 but it is not to be had. Good dreams defy will power.

Still pitch dark, my ears hear the first rooster crow. Still two more crows to go, an hour of sleep remains. At the third crowing, I notice a faint light filtering through the cracks, and the morning ritual of sweeping the dirt clean of debris in front of the house says, "It's time, you sluggard, to rise and shine and get off your Beautyrest mat." Reluctantly I disentangle myself from the net, keeping my feet off the damp earth floor, and search for my sandals. I will need Doans Pills for breakfast. I open the door.

"You sleep well?" comes the ritualistic pre-coffee non sequitur.

"Yes, very well," I lie easily. "And you?"

"No, not too well. You snore."

So I must have slept after all.

PART FOUR
AN ENVIRONMENTAL IMPACT STATEMENT

After all is said and done, the Church declares to her people, ''There is hope laid up for you in heaven that far surpasses the suffering you have known.''

PERSPECTIVE

Missionaries are presented with numerous babies and bodies. Maternity wards on the one hand and Christian funerals on the other have made missionaries a part of the birth and death cycle of the people. An atrociously high infant mortality rate of 40 percent demands a comprehensive, compassionate response. They may not die of heart disease, but they do die of measles, fevers, diarrhea, snake bites, and malaria. Our hospitals have delivered thousands of babies, and the public health programs have succeeded in keeping thousands more away from the hospitals. Institutions of medicine and education are created to meet the needs of the populace, but programs and buildings are not enough.

The system is as good—or as bad—as the people who run it. A hospital, intended as an agent of mercy and an instrument of compassion, can become a dehumanizing chamber. Doctors may be administrators of an endless game of triage: there is not enough for all, so who will live and who will die? Even missionaries can be inadvertently caught up in policies that serve to protect the system first.

"If any one has the world's goods and sees his brother in need, yet closes his heart against him, how does God's love abide in him?" asks St. John (1 John 3:17). The missionary is often found in the position of advocate for someone in need, frequently in antagonism to some system: releasing a worker from jail, paying a fine, or watching over the caregivers. The cup of cold water once given slacks the thirst, then our task continues. For St. John also said, "God gave us eternal life, and this life is in his Son. He who has the Son has life; he who has not the Son has not life" (1 John 5:11,12).

In the end, though, it is still the sting of death that makes humanity walk in fear. No cure, no healing is permanent, except that of the Spirit. After all is said and done, the Church declares to her people, "There is a hope laid up for you in heaven that far surpasses the suffering you have known."

ELEVEN

DANCE AROUND THE CULTURE

Scene: The cavernous blackness of a cloudy night had already fallen on the land when I heard a shuffle of feet and muffled, uncertain voices that always precede a polite cough at the door. Ruth got up to answer. I listened from the inside.

Under the swirl of bugs attracted by the porch light stood six people. A grandmotherly woman was clutching an emaciated little baby to her long, flat breast. A younger woman about six months pregnant stood next to her with the pastor's wife. One step down and behind were two men. Our dispensary and missionary nurses stood to one side.

The scene was now set for a life and death dance around the culture. We were all about to play roles that culture and faith had assigned us.

Missionary Nurse: We've got a problem here. This baby's mother died in an accident several days ago. We can't find a way to feed him.

Ruth: He really looks thin.

Dispensary Nurse: He has been trying to nurse on his grandmother for a week now.

Ruth (in English): Her breasts look like empty wineskins. *(In dialect):* What can we do?

Pastor's Wife: We thought you might have some infant formula for him.

Dispensary Nurse: We don't have any at the dispensary. Our stock of meds is way down.

Ruth: No, I don't have any. Sorry.

Missionary Nurse: I'm sure we could get some from the hospital, but I don't think we should.

Man 1: We need it! She can't produce any milk!

Missionary Nurse: Well, formula needs to be prepared according to the directions. If not, it could kill the baby.

Man 2: We can read the directions. Just explain them to us.

Missionary Nurse: Well, you need to sterilize the bottles each time. If you don't, the formula spoils. If the baby doesn't finish it, you must throw the rest away since you don't have refrigeration. All it takes is one unclean bottle and he could die.

Pastor's Wife: Can you be sure it's sterile every time?

Man 1 (with some hesitation): No, that is doubtful.

Dispensary Nurse: Can you missionaries give them some powdered milk? All you need is just regular water.

Ruth: Yes, we have some. But I don't think that's a good solution, either. We can give you a can, but for the long run you'll have to buy it at the store. One can is a month's salary. Can you afford it?

Man 1: No.

Missionary Nurse: I think it would be best if this young woman nursed him. She is obviously able *(pointing to her ample breasts).*

Young Woman: No, I can't do that.

Missionary Nurse: Why not?

Young Woman: That's not our way.

Missionary Nurse (with some impatience): What's not your way?

Young Woman: We only nurse one at a time. Even twins—our ancestors used to allow one twin to die.

Missionary Nurse: Can't you make an exception to your custom this once?

Young Woman: No, that would kill the baby in my womb.

Pastor's Wife (to the missionary nurse): It's common knowledge that nursing another baby while pregnant often kills the soon-to-be-born baby. Even if it doesn't die in the womb, there won't be enough milk for both babies when it is born.

Young Woman: Besides, I don't have enough milk now anyway.

Missionary Nurse: But it would start. The baby's sucking will make it start! And if you drink lots of fluids and eat well, you will have enough for both.

Pastor's Wife: Can't you find another wet nurse in the village?

Man 1: No, we're not of this tribe. They won't do it, or if they do we can't be sure of what they are really doing to the baby.

Ruth: Who is the baby's father?

Pastor's Wife: He left a long time ago. We don't know where he is.

Missionary Nurse: Well, I'm sure that if she drinks lots of water, she would be able to nurse both babies.

Man 1: No, no. This isn't even our baby. We're not going to risk ours for this one who doesn't even have a father.

Ruth: Maybe you should go to the hospital. They have a "milk baby" program.

Man 2: We could never afford to stay there until he was weaned. We have no family there, and prices are high.

Missionary Nurse: What do you propose, then—just to let him die?

Man 1: It's really up to you, isn't it? We're not afraid of death. We came from the earth and will return to the earth.

Pastor's Wife: This isn't a matter of fearing death, but preserving life.

Ruth: Well, if that's the way it is . . . Grandma, you drink lots of water, maybe you can still nurse after all.

Grandmother: Umph.

Ruth: Drink lots of water all day. *(To the men):* Give her food; maybe she can still do it.

Man 2: Maybe, but it's in God's hands. If he wants it to die, it will.

Pastor's Wife: That's not the way it is. God gave you this child to care for. If it dies, it's because you let it, or your customs make you, or because you cherished money more than the child's life. This death will be on your heads.

Man 1 (Looks for a long time at her, then at the baby. Silence. He takes the baby in his hands and descends the steps. The others follow.): Let's go.

Ruth, Missionary Nurse, Pastor's Wife, Dispensary Nurse: Where are you going? What are you going to do?

The people disappear into the night. The small light of the flashlight bobs down the road until it, too, disappears.

TWELVE
A CLOSE ENCOUNTER OF THE THIRD WORLD

For a few brief moments he held her in his arms and they gazed into each other's eyes. There was no way to fathom what each was thinking and experiencing at that moment. All too quickly, she twisted out of his feeble old arms and bounced away laughing. For a few fleeting seconds there had been an incredible bridge built across a bottomless cultural chasm, between a white-haired African pastor on his deathbed and Rachel, our daughter of nineteen months.

Tata Makuta had come home from the hospital to arrange his affairs. This man had finished Bible school in the early thirties and had been the first Christian witness in many areas. He had come to our area and begun work there when it was still jungle. Soon after his death he would become something of a legend. There seemed to be no end to what he had experienced and suffered in his life. Neither was there any end to the works he had seen God do. Tata's testimony to God's grace and glory was without limiting horizon.

Ruth, Rachel, and I went to visit him before he went back to the hospital. We drove up on our motorcycle, scattering chickens to one side and ducks to the other and arousing Tata from his sleep. His wife came out to greet and usher us into a half-finished hut with a roof and no walls. On the hard reed bed he lay, white beard silhouetted against the light, hands folded across his chest. He sat up as we entered and greeted us. We sat down on the offered chairs.

His bed was close to the fire for warmth. As we talked, he would occasionally poke the fire to keep it going. The smoke curled upwards, filling the conical roof with haze, then drifted out under the thatch. As we sat under the smoky ceiling, the air currents caused a gentle undulation. Rachel played around us, poking the fire, trying to sit on the low-slung "lazy-man" chairs, falling down, laughing, always just out of reach. Then she stumbled near Tata's bed and he picked her up.

For a moment the conversation stopped, Rachel ceased to squirm and they looked at each other. What was it that brought them together? How could this situation even exist? Here was a servant of God, full of hope for the Church of Jesus Christ and his own coming life with his Lord. Here was a hoary old man preparing to die, a personality formed by people, events, mores, and superstitions that no missionary will ever fathom. Then there was Rachel, young, white, female, with the best and worst of life ahead, yet to be formed by her own paradigm of people, events, and beliefs. Suddenly with Rachel's cry, this close encounter of the Third World was broken and she got down. Tata seemed consoled by having held Rachel for a moment.

He seemed tired and lay down again. We felt we were tiring him and offered to go. As if he did not hear us, he began to tell us how the Lord had blessed him in the hospital. He had spoken to many people, leading some to Jesus. In some odd way it reminded me of Samson, who in his final weakened state, worked mightier works by the Spirit of God than in his prime. He talked of what the Lord was presently doing. No past-tense faith, no nostalgic reminiscing of hindsighted years. He was being carried forward to be caught up with the Lord. As we rose to leave, this man whom God had previously healed of tuberculosis and leprosy declared his faith that this time, too, the Lord would save him.

Only the call and impact of the good news of Jesus Christ could have created this situation. His brooding Spirit pushes us outward to cross cultural chasms, repair racial ruptures, and proclaim peace on earth. Watching Tata Makuta with Rachel, my thoughts turned to Simeon, another old man who had held a baby in his arms.

The lordship of Jesus has spanned the ages and straddled the continents. I saw it happen in an old man's lap.

THIRTEEN
MAMA'S NEW HOUSE

She sat on her little stool and stared through the smoky fire into space. Her head still rested on his now lifeless and cooling shoulder. She made no attempt to remove it. "The Lord giveth and the Lord taketh away. Blessed be the name of the Lord." "Bless the Lord, O my soul, and all that is within me bless his holy name." But everything within her wanted to cry and not to bless. The brewing emotions demanded screams and wailing. Platitudes of praise could be true tomorrow but were not so today. Why, God, oh why? She felt herself crumbling as a torrent of sorrow washed away her stoic embankments. She felt sorrow for him and sorrow for herself as she faced what she knew would be a future of destitution.

Then as the last piling eroded and fell away, she flung herself across his wizened body, grown so thin over these months of cancer, and began to sob—first quietly, then more loudly. Soon her grief-laden wails, breaking off as she choked and gasped for air, were heard over the whole village. The first arrivals found her stretched over him, clothes torn, fingers buried in his flesh. The men tried gently to lift her off, but she grasped the body even more determinedly. Then, with forceful resolve, they dragged her off, though she still clung to him, pulling the old body from the bed. Finally, the women put their arms around her and led her away. The intensity of the village's sorrow increased steadily as news of the old preacher's death spread from house to house. The word leaped like a grass fire down the road, causing new incendiary sobs. People moved into the road and grasped each other as they made their way to see the body.

Soon Tata's corpse was surrounded by family, friends, and foes. Each remembered him as they wished. He was the loving father, the concerned husband, the intrepid preacher and man of God. Farmer. Builder. Overseer. He was also the one who put his finger on sin, and by his very upright example created enemies. The wailing would just begin to sub-side when another would arrive reviving their sorrow.

I was on my way back from working on the water pump when I heard the news. I charged through gears of my Honda, horn buzzing at unfortunate goats and children. The sobbing ceased as the motor's ring-ding-ding neared. I pulled up next to the group of mourners and dismounted. A strange apparition at a funeral was I: cut-offs, boots, and a bright red helmet. I walked over and shook a few hands, then observed the body for a few moments. Someone got up and offered me a chair. An uneasy silence fell over the people. I talked a bit with those around me, then went over to where Mama was sequestered. We talked in low tones, then prayed. Everyone chimed in with an "Amen." Remounting, I fired the bike into noisy life and left them in a haze of blue smoke. I had tardily realized how inappropriate was my demeanor. I would come back later.

The wake returned to normal.

A coffin was rapidly prepared and by late afternoon the funeral procession began. First came a few children and young girls waving flowers. Second in order was the casket made from packing crates. Then the pastors, family, and missionaries. Last, stretching a quarter-mile, were the friends and foes. Toward the front they sang Christian songs, led by a pastor. Toward the rear, and mostly out of earshot, they sang ancestral songs of death.

At the grave the line of mourners flowed into itself and formed a sea of people. The service was dignified and brief. The pastor preached a short sermon on the topic, "Happiness Is for the Afterlife." Then the ornate casket marked with various stamps bearing the commercials of "Tomato Paste" and "Pillsbury" was solemnly lowered into the grave. Mama tried to break through but was restrained. A few ceremonial shovels of dirt were tossed on top. After the service Mama walked back, supported by some of the women.

She was the last to return home. The house was a neat little brick structure with a tin roof and a cement floor. It had been built by the mission, and had been their home for the last five years. Behind it was an old cookhouse that seemed to have a terminal disease. The mud walls were falling down, and the grass roof allowed rain to pour in. Near this cookhouse stood a circle of sticks. Tata had begun to build a new cookhouse before he became too weak. He had not been able to finish it. No one had helped.

As she neared her house she saw a few pots and pans and other things carefully arranged in front in three piles. These were her things. As she watched, hardly caring, her brother-in-law came out carrying their table. It went into the pile. Tata's nephew came next and put Tata's gun and radio in the second pile. His niece came out and threw an armload of clothes on the third pile.

One part of her understood what was happening and faintly protested. Most of her was still lost in grief. She had expected it, but still it was not easy. As she watched numbly from her chair, the piles grew. New piles were begun. Tata's family continued to help themselves to his belongings. She owned nothing and had no rights to any of it. They left her a change of clothes and a pot.

When Tata's family left to go home some days later, she moved out of the brick house and into the cookhouse. She had not been asked to, but she did. It was Tata's house, not hers. Soon a teacher and his family moved in after her.

She continued to live in the cookhouse, staring through the holes at the barren circle of Tata's sticks. Well-wishers continued to descend upon her for the next several months. Some stayed days on end. Each expected tea and something to eat. Yet she had nothing. Nothing. Once in a while a missionary would send some tea, food, clothes, even money. The mission was her one lifeline.

The church, I felt, was ignoring her plight and seemed to be saying, "Can't you missionaries do something for her?"

Finally, after much procrastination and delay, I determined to face the pastor with his irresponsibility. Tata, I reasoned, had been a servant of the Lord and not the mission. It was the task of the church to care for its widows. Before going to see the pastor, I went by Mama's cookhouse one more time. Nobody seemed to be around. Odd. I peeked inside. It was empty. I went on to the pastor's house. He met me outside on the porch.

"Hi! Say, are you coming to the dedication?"

"Ah, what dedication?"

"Oh," he looked surprised. "You must not have been told. We've built Mama a new house down near the river in her home village. She couldn't stay in that run-down cookhouse forever, you know."

I knew, all right. Once again I knew too little too late. The mission might have helped her immediate need, but ultimately the security net formed by the church community broke her fall. To see that happen was perhaps Tata's greatest gift.

FOURTEEN
CHILD OF THE COVENANT

Kalombo and his wife, Josephine, walked slowly down the road towards their village. For some reason, Josephine was always called by her European name and never her authentic African one, Kovungbaloma. She carried the large pan piled high with clothes and food down the rough road with consummate grace. Her hips served as a gyroscope, all forward motion neatly distributed by the swaying waist, her head gliding along like a water snake. Her neck muscles stood out and glistened in the midday sun. She had been walking since early morning, but she was not tired. She had carried larger loads than this since her short-lived youth. No, her weary gait was not from the weighty pan, but because of the bundle strapped to her husband's back.

Kalombo trudged along a few paces in front of her, sightlessly staring ahead. Maybe an hour, maybe two, had crept past without a word being spoken. He carried a little suitcase in his right hand, tied together with strips of bark. Upon his back a blanket enveloped a small bundle. This, too, was tied with loops of bark around his shoulders. A reed mat that served as a bed was balanced on his head.

The eyes of the sun high overhead bled their strength like leeches. Finally they stopped under the shade of a baobab tree. Kalombo helped his wife lower the heavy pan to the ground, then unslung his pack as well. They sat on a small log.

"The return trip seems harder, my wife."

"No doubt. We are carrying the same things, but our hope has been extinguished."

"If only we had come sooner, but how were we to know?"

"That's past and done. It was just too far to go."

A silent signal was passed as they rose, took up their bed, and walked. Josephine fell in behind him on the usual short tether. Try as she might, she could not take her eyes off the blanket strapped to her husband's back. Her anguish seemed to rise and fall with the rhythmic movement of her husband's stride. Watching that little package was like rubbing hot peppers into her eyes, which were clouded in pain. What torture could be better devised to break a mother's heart? She was not solaced remembering that three of her five children were still budding in fine growth.

They marched along this way for some time. Then Josephine, lost in her reveries of loss, stumbled over a rock in the road. She tried to regain her balance, but the heavy pan pulled her over and crashed to the ground, spewing their belongings along the road. Stoically cauterizing her bleeding heart, she bent to reassemble their goods.

They stopped at one village and drank some water, but they did not rest. They thanked their host for the drink and continued on. The host wrinkled up his nose after them and made some comment to his wife.

Towards evening they arrived in another village along the way. They decided to ask the village pastor for lodging that night. The church compound served as a hotel for all the Christians traveling that way, and many others besides.

The pastor came out to greet them and bade them sit down while his wife prepared them something to eat. He inquired about their trip, how they were, and how their family was.

"So you came from the hospital. Why did you go there?" he asked.

"Our baby was sick."

"Oh, too bad," he said solicitously. "He has been sick a long time?"

"Yes, several weeks. He wouldn't eat and he had diarrhea."

"Well, why didn't you go sooner?"

"Pastor, we tried several herbs and none worked; the *guérisseur* said that if the baby drank less water the diarrhea would stop, and it seemed to. It's a long two-day walk, and to carry all our belongings, pots, pans, and food for a long stay at the hospital—well, you don't just take off quickly on a trip like that."

"I know," he sighed. "How long did you stay?"

"Only three days."

"That's not long. Did he get better so quickly? I don't see the child; did you leave him with someone there?"

"No."

The pastor sat for a moment, letting the significance of that "no" sink in. A long moment passed. He glanced at the blanket. Now he recognized that odor.

"I am sorry. This is a very sad thing."

A sob escaped Josephine's lips. They all wept silently for a time.

"You are taking him home to be buried." It was a statement, not a question. They all nodded. "It is very far." They all nodded again.

"We must bury him in his own village. . . ." They didn't finish.

"Or else his spirit will not be content?" came the gentle but probing question from the pastor. "My friends, all the earth is God's. Your child will be happy wherever he is buried because his home is with God."

Silence stretched out in the night sounds.

Kalombo thought this was true. He also had the very practical matter of carrying the body another long day in the tropical heat. How neatly this pastor's words had cut through the complicated convolutions of his thoughts.

The next morning when the church gathered for prayer as usual, they conducted a funeral instead. The message restored hope. The person in Christ is certain of his or her resting place in the mansion that Jesus has prepared. Tears are dried. Sorrow is for loss, not for the one lost.

The rest of the trek home was still dry and hard, but Josephine knew that the weight chained to her husband's back and heart was gone. From all outward appearances, nothing had changed. They still toiled along in single file under the sun's glare. But inwardly everything had changed. The blanket was empty and the heart was full.

PART FIVE

FLESHING OUT
THE WORD

*Try as we might, we will never be able to
assume the role of an insider.*

PERSPECTIVE

" . . . In dealing with a 'strange' culture the missionary must simultaneously use two minds, that of the local people and his own."[1] To be able to use the mind of the local people, we must enter that society as learners. Integrative cultural themes, psychological thought processes, and the underlying premises of their logic must become second nature for the missionary.

Try as we might, we will never be able to assume the role of an insider. To the insider belongs the right of innovation. Missionaries as outsiders may advocate change but not make change. "We are commissioned to advocate the allegiance to God that issues in Christian reinterpretation and transformation in the lives and cultures of which we are aware."[2] Our advocacy of change produces only resistance if narrowly aimed at particularly "evil" sins, whether it be begging, drinking, or drugs. Rather, ours is the task of bearing witness as best we can to another worldview, without the accouterments of Western Christianity.

The Gospel is perceived in any culture through its advocate. An attitude and a presence that bespeak Christ become powerful intercessors for change. We are only earthen vessels, often cracked, leaky, and ugly—rarely the beautiful vase destined for glory. It is the mystery and power of God that the Gospel is nevertheless channeled through us.

[1] Louis J. Luzbetak, *The Church and Cultures* (Pasadena, CA: William Carey Library, 1970), p. 169.
[2] Charles Kraft, *Christianity in Culture* (Maryknoll, NY: Orbis Books, 1981), p. 360.

FIFTEEN
MOANU

The little Cessna 180 with the call letters CMU droned along over the river that wound its way into the lush green jungle like a demented python. It twisted and turned below us in kinky convolutions, at times almost doubling back on itself. A mile as the crow flies would take five as the fish swims. Occasionally we would spot a little cluster of huts below, perched alongside the deep, determined river. Specks of humanity would scurry out into the central clearing and wave at the plane.

The pilot pointed to something down below us. At first I did not see it, but then an eruption in the waters' even-flowing surface marked the point of interest. CMU took a dishearteningly steep bank to the left as we spiraled down for a closer look. We came up the river with the wheels skimming the water. The little Cessna took the corners like a bobsled. Two hippos threw up their heads as we roared around a corner on one wing. They were cavorting in the shallows but plunged immediately into the deep channel with a giant splash, and the reddish-brown water quickly hid them in its murky depths.

The plane evened out along one of the few straight stretches. We marveled at the dense jungle: green, green everywhere. What a mindbreaking jigsaw puzzle this scene would make! A few canoes began to appear along the grassy shoreline, a sure sign that we were approaching a village. The fishermen stood and waved as we sped past. At least we left no wake to swamp them.

The village suddenly appeared at my elbow, a small piece of property carved out of the luxuriant brush along the bank. A sandy beach lined a little lagoon. Children splashed and played while their mothers beat the soapy clothes on a semi-submerged log. No doubt they had heard the motor for several minutes before our red wing swept by them. But they were unprepared to see a plane a few yards away. The children scampered out naked and dripping wet and made for their mothers, who, as if in chorus, all straightened up holding the frothy clothes in their hands. None waved, but all stared.

Suddenly the plane went into a steep bank. The village disappeared from view with a stomach-stretching lurch as the little plane gallantly tried to make the corner. But, seeing how that corner continued to tighten, the pilot—wisely in my estimation—let it slide up and out of the river channel and over the trees. The river quickly hid itself among the trees once again. We continued on our journey at 5,000 feet where the green canopy hid whatever human life might exist below it.

From a mile high I let my imagination run over what life must be like in that little village, which I later learned was called Moanu. The pretty little lagoon must provide a continuous source of joy for the children. The tropical sun would keep it warm, the sandy beach a place to frolic and sun oneself. The little stream flowing into the river no doubt was their water source, clear and sparkling and close. Their diet would be fish and wild game, supplemented by bananas and legumes of various kinds; a good, healthy diet that would produce a strong, vigorous people. The possible garden space stretched to the horizon, even from my height, and since they were only two days by canoe from a small town, they could ferry their produce to town for sale. Sacks of corn, wild game, and even coffee would make little Moanu a relatively wealthy village. They would have money to send their children to school or even build one. Some cement and tin roofing would not even be out of the question. A people such as this would be receptive to the Gospel. Because their basic physical needs were assured, they would move up Maslow's hierarchy to more sophisticated spiritual needs, such as art and religion.

I had never put much faith in Maslow's neat little triangle, and Moanu was to turn it topsy-turvy. A few months later I had occasion to stay there.

Two catechist-evangelists and I neared Moanu in our little inflatable Zodiak riverboat. We slid around a bend a little too fast, sending a spectacular wake rolling toward shore. We cut power and coasted in. The boat hit the beach and a kaleidoscope of butterflies swirled up into the air, then settled down on us like locusts. It was deathly quiet. It was unnerving. The normal procedure was for the motor to suck the whole village down to the beach like a vacuum cleaner. Finally, some hesitant children emerged from the bushes and stood watching us. A couple of women and an elderly man also made their appearance.

"Hi!" I said, gulping down a butterfly.

"Greetings," he returned. "We knew you were coming." Somehow.

"We'd appreciate it if we could stay here for a few nights."

"Ummm. Just follow me."

With some relief we loaded most of the gear onto the increasingly brazen children, who with squeals of delight, ran up the hill to the village. We left the boat and motor anchored in the lagoon. Following at a more sedate pace, we noticed the small garden plots along the path, planted with manioc, bananas, and marijuana.

We walked through the village towards what was evidently the head-man's hut. The village was in a sad state of disrepair. The walls were crumbling, the thatch thin and poor, if not porous. A few women were busy pounding manioc, and several old men were stripping the leaves from the dried marijuana plant. Children sat and watched the spectacle go by.

The headman settled us under a shaded tree and ordered the child-porters to stash our gear in a little hut nearby. One by one the villagers gathered round to see what was afoot.

My evangelical olfactory sense quickly detected the presence of strong drink. Several of the people had come with jugs of a murky white liquid. Then, as we sat and talked informally, inquiring about their families and health, we were introduced to a most horrible little village. My misty visions of idyllic life quickly evaporated under truth's glare.

A suckling babe whimpered, and instead of treating him to mother's milk, they laughingly poured a generous amount of the palm wine into a cup and persuaded the babe to drink many mouthfuls. Soon the mother was unable to hold him any longer because of her own growing inebriation and sat him on the ground. His unstable little body weaved a moment, then he plopped right on his face. They all laughed.

The jug went around again.

The only person that could be characterized as a "young man" engaged me in conversation. I listened attentively to several minutes of non-stop gibberish. I occasionally caught a word, even a coherent fragment, but the message was lost in this oral Rorschach test. At the close he evidently asked me a question. When I did not answer, another tried to explain what he had said, with better but still meager results. Finally I understood that he wanted me to perform a Christian marriage ceremony for him and his wife to prevent her from deserting him. I declined as gracefully as I could.

I warmed up to one relatively sober woman, who turned out to be the sister of a deacon whom I knew upstream.

"Where are all the young men?" I asked, supposing wrongly that they were all off hunting.

"Oh, gone." She gestured vaguely. "They leave here as soon as they can, it seems."

"Then who works the gardens and huts?"

"The young girls do, and we do," she said pointing at the worn group gathered around. As I had seen few girls, I guessed—this time correctly—that they were out working the gardens.

"But the girls leave, too. They marry up and down the river." I had indeed met a couple of Moanu girls upstream. The river people were in reality one giant, complex web of criss-crossing relations.

The village was plainly dying. No youth, no enterprise except drugs, a bare subsistence diet eked out by a few girls and old people. Education? A few went to a school about four hours away. That school terminated at fourth grade. All were fogged out by palm wine.

The village headman spoke up.

"The last time *fumus* [Protestants] came here, we wouldn't let them stay," he cackled at us meaningfully. "We got our church already. We are already children of God." He pointed at the tiny dilapidated building. "So what do you want?"

Everyone in the village was there now, in one state or another. Taking a deep breath I launched into an explanation of the Gospel that I hoped would make some sense in these befuddled heads. I did all right until I swept my eyes around the crowd. My stream of thought broke over the shoals of the drunken baby lying in the dirt. The coming of Christ and his atonement for sins seemed to wash up on the beach like so much foam. I made myself say things about victory over sin and getting to heaven, ending with a personal testimony. The two catechists also spoke and gave their testimonies. The jug, now emptied, was tossed on the ground like a period to our meeting.

"Well, you can stay," the headman said, squinting at the setting sun. I had not known it was still a matter of question. Our testimonial service must have "passed."

We sat around our fire and sang and talked until late at night. Then realizing that our hosts were waiting for us to retire before they did, we graciously went into the house. After praying together too perfunctorily for a good night's sleep, we quickly settled down under our nets.

The difference between the airplane view of this idyllic little village and the reality of its sordid existence is ever with me. Ministry from a mile high crashed quickly after an encounter with the tendrils of Satan. Over the next years I had occasion to come again and again to these river villages. Yes, they traffic in drugs and palm wine. Many are captivated by Satan and his ruses. But several churches have been planted, and the branches of the mustard tree have continued to spread. The arrival of the Gospel fanned into flames yearnings that had for years been numbed by palm wine and marijuana. In Christ, some dared to hope again for a better life here below and eternal life above.

SIXTEEN
THE FALLEN VIRGIN

Bravo for authenticity!'' The enthusiastic shouts of the crowd rolled like a wave over the city. The strident voice of the country's leader carried to every hut and every little stall in the market. "We seized our national independence years ago," he cried, "but we still are in cultural slavery. Though we elect our own officials, we are in danger of forgetting that we are not Europeans but Africans! Let us find our roots; let us recover our heritage; let us drop the Western mask and be authentic Africans. Authenticity bravo!"

The eyes of the people were opened to cultural oppression. They began to observe their town with a different perspective. Symbols of cultural pollution were discovered everywhere. Colonial mansions stood out in a defiance of stucco and brick. Behind the counters of the largest stores sat not blacks but whites. Street names were "Avenue of Paris" or "Boulevard of Woods." The citizens became cognizant that their own names of Joseph and Robert were given them out of futile imitation of an enemy. The bank with its sweeping entranceway and guarded vaults spoke of wealth removed from their lands. Schools used Western tomes glorifying the West, while a scant few chapters described the African poverty of history and culture.

The palm-lined road inevitably led past the Catholic church. Its cathedral stared at them through stained-glass eyes, and its spires rose above their palm trees. White priests enforced a celibacy that split the even flow of the African life-current like a mud-mired snag. At the entrance to the compound stood the thin-lipped Virgin in white. Her hands were held demurely before her, long flowing hair cascading down her back. Where was the African Madonna?

Wild emotions spun around and round, fed by the wine of "FREE-DOM!" The crowd began to surge through the streets. Signposts went down. Stores were hastily padlocked shut by their fleeing proprietors.

The crowd moved past the bank to the church and stood before the Virgin. As "Bravo for authenticity!" split the air, they grappled with the towering statue. At first she refused to give in. New ropes were tossed over her head, and other strong arms gave assistance. Finally she began to break. Iron rods were pulled out of reinforced concrete by sheer force. She crashed to the ground, and a jubilant shout arose. The Virgin had fallen and now lay crumpled on her back before them.

But, wait, what is this? First one, then another began slapping their arms and face frantically. Those nearest the Mother tried desperately to escape the frenzied hornets. In their desperation they turned and trampled over those behind as the angry, buzzing cloud issued from the Madonna's broken body. They covered their heads and ran.

The next day, several well-protected youths came and gathered the succulent honey.

Two years later she remained exactly where she had fallen. The street names had changed. Black faces were behind the store counters and in the cathedral. Yes, there had been progress. Yet the reach for authenticity and freedom would continue until the whitewashed Virgin sprawled on the ground was sculptured black and stood again on her feet.

SEVENTEEN
OPEN PALM

Two grotesque feet filled my whole frame of vision. The disheveled beggar was speaking, but his hideous feet drowned out his words. Never had I seen anything like them before. Like gnarled old tree boils, they fastened themselves on the end of his legs. His feet did not belong to him. Dirty strips of cloth wound around this way and that, apparently binding his rotting, putrefying flesh together. I could only spot the open sores when the flies were momentarily thrown off balance by a movement. I gave him some bread and he went away. Two dark, damp spots marked where he had stood.

A few days later he was back. This time I managed something resembling a conversation before I gave him his due. A huge smile and warm handshake transmitted an overly enthusiastic thanks.

On several occasions I tried to talk with him about Jesus. He believed in Jesus. He went to mass. But all the while his two leprous feet made me wince at my own words. Here was a man I felt to be orbiting just beyond my possible field of ministry. There was nothing with which I could reach him. His two leaky lumps sneered at my faith, which was equal only to praying for colds and safe trips.

This monotonous mendicancy went on for several months. One day, however, he arrived on a bicycle. Not an old, homemade fabrication, but a nice new shiny one with two rearview mirrors and a horn. He dismounted and came over for his week's money.

"Who lent you the bike?" I queried.

"Nobody. I bought it."

The ensuing silence finally propelled him to add, "So I can make my rounds faster."

That was the last day he begged from me. I gave him his walking papers. I fired him as my beggar. I would hire another one who acted more like a beggar ought to act. A new bicycle, indeed! Beggars walked or crawled; they didn't ride on their own bikes!

That was also the day a new decree went out from the Caesar Augustus of that African nation that beggars could only beg on Saturdays. It was counter-revolutionary to beg on Tuesday morning or Friday noon. So on the next Saturday and on every Saturday since I found a large group of beggars at my door. I had traded one for many, it seemed. This group evidently met in town and traveled on a group discount from house to house. In the back I noticed my friend the leper. He walked with the itinerant beggars. Evidently he discovered that his bike was counter-productive.

"Do you want to be healed?" Jesus asked.

The most frequent answer to that question is "No." My friend the beggar, I have since learned, has refused to go to the hospital for treatment and even rejects the "shoes" someone tailor-made for him.

What do you do with someone whose answer to the question is a consistent and resounding, "No"? Day after day I pass their Bethsaida pool. My shallow repertoire of responses is inadequate to answer the professional manipulation of guilt.

At times I have flatly said no and turned away from their open hand. Other times I have given them what they requested with a blessing. I have offered them work, and even prayed for their healing in spite of themselves. No tactic succeeded in moving them beyond the open palm.

By chance one day I was talking with a fellow who knew this notorious leper. He told me with a disgusted snort that he was a relative of the town's chief. Even though the clan was well off financially, they sent him out to beg.

Oddly enough, this made me more empathetic with his plight. He was under enormous clannish pressures. He was the outcast, the disenfranchised cousin, exchanging begged goods for toleration in the clan. Fresh currents of agape blew through my new window of understanding.

PART SIX

THEY FOLLOWED HIM TO SCHOOL ONE DAY

The Christian churches are responsible for educating six million children. Ours is the assignment to do it well.

PERSPECTIVE

Formal institutional education is both a consequence and a cause of rapid modernization in Africa. Abilities in literacy, mathematics, and European languages are key to advancement and healthy salaries. Whenever a child demonstrates an academic gift, family and friends are plenteous and generous with the child whose abilities may someday repay them many times over.

It is also a cause of cultural discontinuity: the purposes of Western education are entirely different than those of traditional societies. Though they have no formal schools, tribal societies educate their children by enculturation. They seek to produce continuity in their culture. They want their children to follow the traditions of the ancestors and elders. Their informal system of education seeks recruitment and maintenance—recruitment to membership in the tribe and to specific tasks and roles; maintenance of values, beliefs, and skills that maintain the society.

Western education, to the contrary, seeks to make "progress," a dearly elusive term. Whatever it means, it means succeeding generations are hoped to be "better" than the former. Schools are future oriented, gears to produce graduates adept in the ways of a system just emerging—or not yet in existence.

Most of the schools rose out of the mission enterprise. In 1974 the schools were nationalized, but they returned to church hands in 1977. The Christian churches are responsible to educate six million children. Ours is the assignment to do it well. The gathering of these students is an unparalleled opportunity for the Church and missions.

But there is a foreign flavor on the tongue. The stresses and strains that push and pull on the missionary-educator can lead to real disequilibrium. Often we feel like we are standing on a broken ice pack, a leg on each float. The demands of the institution drift apart from the exigencies of the culture. The sight can be humorous, but few manage to keep the floats together. They opt for one or the other—or fall in.

EIGHTEEN
LIFE LIVED IN THE DAY
OF A PREFET

The national church was looking for someone to fill the office of *préfet*. A *préfet* corresponds loosely to a principal in North America, but here takes a place among a host of minor deities. As such, the *préfet* must have certain qualities of mental toughness. I qualified because I survived two years of Mr. Rogers with hardly a scar, though I speak more slowly. I cut Rebecca's umbilical cord without benefit of clergy. When they opened my dossier, it shrieked *"préfet"* at them.

The first petitioner usually arrives before I leave for school. I have tried leaving earlier, but they are always there. I leave at 5:57 a.m. School is two minutes from home. (I hate commuting and am thinking of moving closer.) When I get out the door, I look both ways for speeding centipedes and army ants. I also look both ways for students. Before I am to the bottom of our five steps, I have accumulated several *préfet* groupies.

"I need to go home."

"The pen you gave me doesn't write."

"The secretary isn't coming today. He has tuberculosis."

That stopped me for a moment in my head-down rush for the office. "T.B.?" I asked. No, he wasn't sure exactly what it was; maybe just a cough.

"I need to go home."

"Why?"

"My father is in prison for something."

"I didn't get my weekly ration allowance."

"My mother's only son died," he said.

There is occasionally a phrase that doesn't sound quite right. "What? How can that be?"

"I don't know either," he said. "Read the letter."

I read it. Sure enough, he was dead. "Oh, you mean your aunt or her other son . . . no, you mean her first son, not 'unique' son." French adjectives!

The only way to escape was to ring the school bell. I could not find the tire iron to beat against the wheel rim hanging from a vine outside the door.

"A student took it to nail his trunk together," volunteered one.

"Lemme help you," said another. He hit it with a stick. It sounded more like engine knock than a school bell.

The students lined up for flag raising. The flag was in a heap at the bottom of the pole. It was kind of hard to salute it. We all stood around and wondered what to do. Finally I seized the initiative; that is what I am paid to do.

"Why can't we raise it?" I demanded.

"The stick is missing."

"Yeah, the primary school kids took it to knock oranges out of the grapefruit trees." They have a hard time with French fruits. I guess we all do.

"Go to class," I said, cleverly resolving the situation.

Nobody moved.

I sighed.

"The doors are still locked."

The secretary had left with the keys to the room. Somebody somewhere had told me that he had T.B. and was not coming, but my memory was cloudy.

"Go in the windows."

Then all the class climbed in over the windows. It did not matter that the first one over had opened the door from the inside.

I settled in behind my impressive desk. It is impressive because it is raised up on three bricks. Anyone sitting on the other side can hardly see over it. Nobody can sit on the corner because there are only three bricks.

The first task of the morning was to find three students who had not spent the night in the boy's dorm. I dispatched my *huissier* to find them. I sent the "custodian" to find a new flag stick. The morning was humming along.

The director of the dormitory came in. He said that so and so had spilled a can of palm oil last night. He had told him to wash the floor of the whole room. He had refused. I sent for so and so, the director left, so and so came in.

"Go wash the dorm floor," I said.

"It is not my turn," he said.

"I don't care; you messed it up, you wash it."

"Messed it up?"

"You spilled the oil can last night and the floor smells. Go wash it!" I said, with some emphasis to underscore my authority.

He started out the door. "I didn't spill it, but I'll go wash it if you want; but they are having a test this hour and. . . ."

The light clicked on. "Aren't you so and so?"

"No. I just came to return the key to the classroom. Here."

I looked at it. Anybody can make a mistake.

"I'm sorry," I said, mustering as much insincerity as I could.

There were serious items on the agenda, too: expel a student who entered with falsified report cards. I had found several such cases; each had compelling reasons stemming from the economic suffering prevalent in the country. Still, it was illegal. They all àsked to stay in class, even to be demoted a class. They begged forgiveness. I expelled them all. Mentally tough, hard as nails. I felt like crying each time. Did I do right?

One of the girls had accused another of having an evil spirit. Others had picked it up as truth. She had "eaten" their souls during the night. They were going to get some poison and finish her off. I spent some time with them in counsel and prayer.

"The math professor needs chalk."

"The French professor wants the attendance sheet."

"The physics prof wants to know why the bat droppings were not swept up this morning."

The bat droppings! I knew there was something I had forgotten.

"I would like to register for the senior year."

I looked up, deadpan.

"You're two months late."

"Well, not really; I was in another school, but they just raised their prices from 500 francs to 3,000 francs yesterday and. . . ."

"They sextupled their price in one day?"

"Yes. That's the day the value of the franc fell from 6:1 to 30:1. They're just keeping even, they say."

"We're not."

"Not what?"

"Keeping even," I said. I would not let him in because where there is smoke, there is smolder. Soon a dozen students fleeing that school came and went.

"*Préfet*," said the direttor of the dorm, "red ants are eating the students at night!"

"Eating. You mean biting?" I said hopefully. French verbs. I said I would think of something.

"We need more bunks; they are sleeping two and three to a bed right now."

I said I would think of something.

I went out to go home for breakfast. I saw by the dawn's early light that the flag was still there in a heap. I heard footsteps coming up behind me. I speeded up, too late.

"Do you have a magazine cover for my books?"

Yes, I did.

I glanced in the church as I walked by. One of our classes meets in there because we lack classroom space. They had stacked pews on top of each other for writing tables. One precariously perched table fell over and clobbered the whole first row.

I nearly made it to the door. Breakfast was inches away. The door is like the altar of mercy in the tabernacle. They don't get me in there. I reached for the door when a figure stepped in front of me.

"*Préfet*, there's a letter from you."

"From me? You mean for me?" French prepositions. I tried to reach around him for the door.

"For you."

I surrendered, and opened the letter.

"It's from you," I said.

"Yes," he said smiling. I read it. It said, "I would like to work in your yard in the afternoons. . . ."

"We'll see," I said, finally opening the door. I got inside.

Breakfast was interrupted only by someone who wanted to borrow our bicycle, a student wondering if his father had sent him some money, and the radio log book.

I had three classes to teach that day. I had begun the first when I noticed a pair of eyes peering at me through the broken windows. My students were busy for the moment so I went to the window.

"Yes?" I whispered.

"Nothing," he whispered back.

"Fine."

Actually I am rarely interrupted in class. Only the military dares interrupt me in class. I looked out of the broken window to see; was it a half-track? No, just a seventeen-ton six-wheel-drive military transport vehicle grunting down our little driveway, squashing the hedge on each side. It stopped by my office.

"Finish reading Genesis 10," I said, "about going whither he knowest not."

The paracommandos jumped down and lounged against the vehicle. The commander came up to me. No doubt I had expelled his only— or first—son.

"You the *préfet*?" he asked.

I tried to read his eyes before answering. I also tried a variety of answers.

"Just temporarily," I said. Beads of perspiration dotted my forehead.

"I brought my son's stuff. Where shall I leave it?"

I sighed with relief. "In the dorm." I gestured somewhere, not sure exactly where it was. Then a thought struck me. "Do you have something for ticks?"

He looked at me strangely. "You have ticks?"

"Ants, I mean ants (French bugs!), to kill ants in the dorm."

He just happened to have some chlorine. I knew I would think of something. The half-track or whatever it was backed out of the path and left. I went back to the office.

"We are out of soap," a student told me.

"What! I supplied the depot with a hundred bars yesterday."

He shrugged. It was not his place to explain the metaphysics of soap to me. I would send more.

"We need notebooks for art class."

"The geography teacher wants to know if you have any geography books for the students—and for him—yet."

"No."

Two teachers came in. They are both teaching thirty-six hours a week and would like to drop a couple of hours. We need more teachers, they said.

The French teacher came in. Would the school pay for a table and chair for his little home? No funds, sorry.

The dormitory director came in again. Could we buy some extra reed beds so they would not have to sleep two to a bed?

And so it went. I will not tell all.

It started raining in the afternoon. I walked by the girl's dormitory under my umbrella. I was under it, that is. I glanced inside. They were all standing up.

"Why are you all standing up?" I asked the obvious question.

"Because it is raining."

What? Had I come upon a new rite, a vestige of yesteryear's paganism, homage to the rain god?

"It's raining inside," they said.

The roof was leaking so badly they had to stand between the rivulets of water.

I went home and started work at my desk. The rain tends to keep the traffic down. But soon my sixth sense told me I was being watched. I tried not to notice but finally looked up. A student stood outside my office in the pouring rain. He had a banana leaf over his head.

"I came to get the soap for the depot."

I gave him a new box of soap.

Another cough:

"Yes?"

"I have a spiritual problem."

Ah, now we are talking. This is what I went to seminary for, why I am in missions.

"Please come in and sit down. Let's start from the beginning. Would you like to tell me about it? You can trust me. Go ahead, be honest."

"Would you sell me a Bible?"

Is that all? Yes, I sold him one. I wanted to ask him in good Rogerian fashion how he felt about that.

But all this is mere child's play for someone who once outwaited a bureaucrat in his own office. Really, I did. I also filled out one form forty-four times for the government. But there was one last straw.

The rain came again, hard. It was dark and somber. I decided to take a shower. I opened the curtain a little to let the light in. I was all lathered up when that squeezy sensation laid hold of me. I turned against my will and looked through the curtain crack at somebody. He still had the banana leaf on his lead. He adjusted it so that the water ran off against the screen.

"Do you want me?" I inquired politely.

"Almost," he said.

"Almost? You mean 'maybe' or 'yes' or what do you mean?" French adverbs again.

He held up the soggy flag. "You forgot to bring the flag in from the rain."

I gave him my best rockets red glare.

I took the next day off. But it was Sunday anyway.

NINETEEN
THE PRICE IS RIGHT

Two uniformed soldiers, one armed, both impeccably dressed, knocked on our door. They courteously introduced themselves and asked if they could come in. We settled down in our chairs.

"I think you know why we've come," was his opening gambit.

I shuffled out a pawn to draw fire. "I'm not really sure, no."

He smiled as he slashed his bishop across my lines. "You expelled the major's son. He would like you to reconsider."

I reconsidered. For the fourth time. The pressure was escalating. First, a personal note from the major politely asking that a second chance be given. Then came a blunt and forceful letter from a political official. Each request had been met with an agony of indecision. Was I simply being stubborn? Upholding some American principle of noninterference and Christian behavior? Yet the church often places missionaries in such positions exactly because they are more able to resist certain pressure and uphold the standards the national church keenly desires.

With each appeal, I had reconvened the disciplinary committee. Each time the original decision had been upheld. He was to be expelled permanently. Finally the major himself had come, dressed in civilian attire, to beg our grace. He left dissatisfied. Evidently the time for pussyfooting around was over.

"We have explained the situation to him. I'm sure we were very clear," I said.

"You were clear; let us also be clear. We will not let you ruin this boy's life."

"He ruined it without any help from me. This is a Christian school. They all signed a statement agreeing to conform to our stipulations. He was warned. This comes as no surprise to anyone."

"What is surprising is your lack of grace. Give him hard labor as punishment, or a temporary exclusion, but allow him back in. This is his senior year!''

"We gave him hard labor. He had to dig a three-meter-deep outhouse in hardpan. We tried provisional exclusion. He finally gave us no choice. He has a long history of recalcitrance that goes back to last year."

Disrespect for the staff had grown into open disobedience. In-hours were mocked. Abusive language characterized his speech. He had even boldly entered a professor's house in broad daylight and removed some articles. He drank. On a lark, he had profited from a professor's absence by teaching a lower class a lesson on sex education, complete with chalk drawings. Each infraction had been met with counsel and stringent sanctions. Perhaps I had been too lenient. I wanted to allow him every opportunity to change. I also knew whose son he was. However, a drunken brawl was finally too much. My staff of national teachers and the pastor encouraged me to expel him. Had it not been for their continued insistence, I probably would let him in again for one more try.

"He will change this time. The major gave him a good talking to."

"Sounds like Eli."

"Who?"

"Somebody in the Bible. I'm sorry, but the decision stands. If I allowed him back in, discipline would be up for grabs. He chose this school; now he can choose another."

"It's too late. He will have to miss the rest of the year and register next year. The major said he would send him off to the army unless you let him back in. You don't want to send him to the army, do you?"

"What the major decides to do with his son is up to him."

"Simbi, your student, has even been hospitalized. Your expulsion threatens his health. He hasn't eaten in days."

"The consequences of one's sin often engenders remorse." I was determined not to shoulder any of the guilt tax for his future or health.

He changed tactics. "You teach a God of grace, but I don't think you know anything about it. A father of grace would have a child of grace."

That was a familiar thrust, but one I had never learned to parry. There was enough truth on the point to draw blood. I feinted.

"Law and grace go together. The wages of sin is death. Simbi never recognized his sin sufficiently to avail himself of grace." The answer was theological enough to confuse him. I had not gone to seminary for nothing.

"So, O.K., what do you want, to let him in again?"

Persuasion had bloomed into bribery. He was careful with his language, though. It could never be proven that bribery was his intention. In fact, I was not really sure myself. How high could I go? Enough to build a new dormitory? Buy new books? Import an evangelist?

"All I want is to create a Christian milieu in which our students can meet the Lord and grow up in the Faith." My answers were beginning to sound a bit pious even to my own ears.

He moved his queen.

"We will be checking traffic this week."

He did not need to draw any pictures. Our driver's licenses were at that moment sitting on his desk waiting for validation. Insurance papers had not yet come through. There were always irregularities in the paper work. Usually these minor lapses were passed over. They could also be used.

Check.

"I understand," I said, wishing I did. Maybe it was not a threat at all, but just a piece of information. We all stood up. "Thank the major for his understanding, too."

We went to the door. "Oh yes," I said, "tell him that his son can come get his academic dossier that I still hold. . . ." I bit my tongue. I was about to say, "if I can find it." At this critical juncture, the loss of the dossier containing his original—and probably only—report cards from primary through high school could devastate his chances of ever getting into another school. Better not to engage in a power struggle with the grand master. I would be sure to lose the contest. I did not want to die by the sword.

However, the implicit threat was not lost on the soldier. "Yes, I'll send him immediately to get them, Monsieur." We shook hands. In spite of the topic of conversation, I was impressed with this man, who with cool aplomb and the utmost courtesy—without the exchange of an angry word—had managed to unlimber a formidable arsenal of guilt, bribery, theology, and power. A soldier he was.

Several days later I had occasion to be in town and my heart was in my throat watching for traffic checkpoints. I was sure Operation Dragnet had been put into operation the moment their outpost saw me coming. I went to the major's office to get our driver's licenses. The secretary gave me a start. He was the major's emissary who had visited our home. He smiled as he handed the licenses over, no doubt amused at my transparent attempts to look unflappable.

"The major says thanks for the dossier."

Now I understood. By the skin of my teeth I had met threats with grace and not counterthreats. Had I touched that dossier, my king would have been captured. By returning it I had returned also the possibility of salvage, of a second chance of grace.

TWENTY
HIGH-RISE FAITH

Dr. Jamo Fa Waluala Gbanyo, graduate of a prestigious European university, director of academics at one of the Christian high schools in Africa, stopped between two classrooms. The high, open windows kept student attention from without while allowing fresh breezes in. The stark cement walls brought the words of the two missionary teachers clearly to his ears. In Room 3 a young woman was teaching social studies to a junior class. Her husband was teaching philosophy to a senior class next door.

"Compare the birth rates on the graph on page 79," she said. "Which country is the lowest?"

A long uncomfortable silence ensued.

"No, no, look again at this syllogism!" her husband shouted in frustration. "What is the major premise?"

"Socrates is a man."

"No, all men are mortal! That is the premise, *all men!*"

"The United States," finally came the reply from Room 3.

"Good, good. Remembering what we just learned about America, why would it be so low?"

"So if all men are mortal, and Socrates is a man—that's the minor premise and there can be many minor premises, which are always more specific than the major—then what is the conclusion?"

"They can't have babies like us, their women have become too weak."

"American women certainly can have babies! Just look at the graph of thirty years ago. The average family size has diminished. Why? Why do they have smaller families?"

"Socrates is mortal."

"Yes, yes, fine. Now look at this. 'All men are mortal, an animal is mortal, therefore. . . .' "

"An animal is a man."

Dr. Jano shook his head. How would his people ever amount to anything? This was just elemental philosophy! Logic was essential to progress.

A cough from a student.

"Yes?"

"Family size is decreasing because people live in high-rise apartments."

"What leads you to make that conclusion?"

"An animal can't be a man, no matter what his syllogism says!"

"It doesn't say that! The minor premise must borrow from the specific term in the major premise. Look at these circles."

Dr. Jano winced at the squeaking chalk.

"Here is the circle of mortals. It's the biggest. Here's the circle of men; it's entirely inside, smaller, more specific. Other categories also fit in the larger circle that aren't men. Your faulty premise always produces faulty conclusions."

"A big circle of mortals?"

"Well, there isn't as much air up there; it's harder to breathe."

"Sanoko, that's really strange! No, that's not it! Listen! America wants to limit family size because large families are too costly."

Dr. Jano agreed wholeheartedly. His eight children attended expensive private schools in town.

"If you please, Professor. I don't understand your premise. In fact, it seems we hardly ever do. We can't understand what you are telling us because we just don't seem to have the same starting point. Do you want to know our major premise?"

TWENTY-ONE
SIGNS OF WITHDRAWAL

T he superintendent of schools asked me if I would go with him to the bank to help withdraw the funds for March salaries. Our account had been credited, permitting us to pay the 300 teachers. We moved together toward the little Toyota Hi Lux crew cab.

"Why's that trunk in the back of the pick-up?" I asked him.

"To carry all the money." Evidently he had known all along that I would agree to help.

I chuckled and quipped, "Are you sure it's big enough?"

"Probably not," he didn't quip.

We climbed in and started off for the first and only bank in town.

"Stop here!" he ordered. He jumped out and came back carrying a large steel drum.

"For money, right?" I divined.

"Yep." He looked at me as if I had never made a withdrawal before.

We carried the trunk and barrel into the bank lobby. A dozen people were lined up ahead of us with their trunks, barrels, and gunnysacks. We drew a number and waited. I sat down and sank into my somnolent state of semiconsciousness that I save for occasions such as this. I was just winning the Boston Marathon when the sup ungraciously woke me out of my reverie. The laurel wreath would have to wait.

"It's our turn."

I walked over to the window marked "Withdrawals" expecting the teller to count the money into my hand. Instead he opened the counter top and ushered us behind. With a weary smile he said, "Let's start." Behind the counter were stacked about a hundred banded metal trunks. He snapped the bands on one and opened it. It was filled with bills. We dumped them onto the floor and began to stack the neatly tied bricks, ten long, ten wide, five deep. Five hundred bricks of money. The bank clerks scurried back and forth with accounts and receipts, stepping over us and our hoard with practiced aplomb.

"How much is this?" I asked when the hour's work was done.

"About 50,000."

"And how much do we need?"

"600,000."

We sprung the bands on another trunk and repeated the process, filling in another large square on the bank floor. The clerks had to hop over one, then the other. Once we had the process down to a science, we could snap the bands, empty the trunk, stack and count it in twenty minutes. We had to space the piles so the clerks could play Wall Street hopscotch. The bank had many vaulters. Finally, we stood at the end of the bank and admired our checkered patterns, with colorful clerks hopping and skipping about. Suddenly our little trunk and barrel seemed woefully inadequate. The banker came up and we signed out the money.

"Well," said the sup, "Let's put it in the truck."

"How?"

"Oh, yes, how, well, we'll borrow these trunks back."

It was a shame to dismantle our engineering handiwork, but we finally stuffed it all back in the same trunks we had just taken it out of. The bank personnel helped us move the trunks out the back door to our truck. I loaded the first trunk into the back.

The banker rushed up, arms waving. "No, no, no, you can't have those trunks! Those belong to the bank!"

"We'll bring them back tomorrow" I protested, looking as honest as possible.

"No, empty them. It's closing time."

I wondered if being a missionary, a pastor, or a Covenanter would persuade him.

"As a missionary . . . " I began.

We dumped the trunks out onto the gravel behind the bank. The trunks were hauled back in and doors clanged shut. The sup started tossing the bundles of cold cash into the back of the pick-up. I was horrified.

"Wait, you can't do that! You can't just drive through the middle of town that way!"

"We'll take a back route then."

"Better to stack it all in the crew cab." So we did. We filled up the back seat from the floor to the ceiling. I had to admire the view in the window. But half the money was still on the ground. Again the bundles were tossed into the back.

The night watchman, a machine-gun toting commando, came on duty at that moment. I saw him as he came around the corner, ready to spend a long, boring night in his easy chair. He glanced up at us and paused. He straightened his shoulders and shifted the weight of the rifle, striding over to us as we furtively tossed money into the truck.

"Act natural," whispered the sup.

He watched us for a long time without comment. His mental process probably went something like this: It is after hours. They are loading the truck with money. They might be robbing the bank. But, the doors are shut and locked. It is broad daylight. They are acting normally. They can't be robbing the bank. So they are either doing this legally or are extremely dangerous, cool customers. Especially the white man who looks like a mercenary I met in Biafra with that beard and all. In neither case do I wish to get involved. Nevertheless, it's my job. . . .

He came closer and peered in the cab window. "Toss me another brick, sup." I said naturally.

"Hey," cried the commando, "What are you doing?"

"Loading this money into the truck," the sup replied. I decided to leave the talking to the sup.

The soldier chewed on that for a moment, walked around to look at the growing mound in the back and diminishing pile on the gravel. Finally that bit of non-information trickled down his nervous system.

"Why?"

The sup sighed, and put his hands on his hips. "We can't just leave it here on the ground, now can we?" He was explaining the ABCs to a schoolboy.

Getting into the swing of this dialogue, I added, "You know how long it would take to move it by wheelbarrow?"

He looked at me speculatively for a moment, unsure whether I was being smart or just stupid. We kept loading. The guard picked up a brick and examined it closely. He held his year's pay in one hand.

"How do I know you're not stealing it? Show me your authorization!"

With a sinking feeling I realized that the receipt that had been on top of the first trunk we unloaded was now buried in the cab.

"Where's yours?" snapped the sup. He wasn't the sup for nothing.

"But I'm the guard," he protested.

"That's what you say. How do I know?"

The next-to-last brick was tossed in. "Get in and start the truck." Then, telling the guard, "Listen, we gotta go," he casually took the brick out of his hand and tossed it into the back. He jumped into the already moving truck, and we eased the Japanese Brinks out of the parking lot. The guard watched us leave, still unsure whether to shoot or not.

"We aren't stopping for anything, Hill," the sup said unnecessarily. We raced through town at "top" speed to prevent anyone from jumping in. Alan Funt should have been there to capture the expressions of people along the road as they watched a Hi Lux of money roar past with a demented missionary at the wheel. They gestured, waved, ran after us. One woman tripped over her long skirt, pulled it down around her knees, and fell into a ditch.

All the school directors were waiting for us at the church, each with a large sack. We stuffed their sacks like Christmas stockings, feeling a little like St. Nick, and away they trudged to their respective schools to pay their teachers. Finally, our sleigh was empty. We said our good-byes and I drove home.

Drive-in banking still had room for improvement.

PART SEVEN
IN . . . BUT NOT OF

God is the redeemer and transformer of cultures.

PERSPECTIVE

I am, in anthropological jargon, a "participant/observer" of my host culture. On the one hand, incarnational ministry results in emotional grafting to the people. The missionary internalizes their hopes, joys, and anxieties. On the other hand, missionaries can never become true insiders. Missiologist Charles Kraft is fond of saying, "We were born of the wrong mother." We are invited to leave the cold shadows of clinical detachment and sit with them by their fire. But the sense of participation in partnership quickly evaporates when the red-hot coal is passed to us. Suddenly, the status of observer seems more desirable.

The balance between these two roles is delicate, and rarely is the equilibrium to our liking. Whether to be participant or observer is not always a matter of choice. Many times I have set out determined to be aloof, detached, and self-protective only to have the shield shattered and my "status" stripped. On other occasions I have been forced to watch helplessly as events ground down to their inevitable conclusion. The culture often defines the balance for us: this far, but no further.

There is so much that is undeniably attractive in the host culture that at times we want to be absorbed totally into it. One can easily appreciate their limitless commitment to family and clan, the patient long-suffering and even joy with which they bear tremendous burdens of death and suffering. However, there is also the inevitable streak of cruelty and corruption that is like hard granite to our desire to drill deeply.

Though God is the judge of all people, including our own, he through Jesus is also the redeemer and transformer of cultures. Donald McGavran states, "As men of each culture become disciples of Christ and responsible members of his church, feeding on his Word and measuring themselves by his revelation, the culture they have inherited and are changing and transmitting moves closer to God's will for it."[1]

We are all in this world, but not of it.

[1] Donald McGavran, *The Clash Between Christianity and Cultures* (Washington, D.C.: Canon Press, 1974), p. 12.

TWENTY-TWO
'LIKE FIRE . . . LIKE A HAMMER'

The gospel team, consisting of African students from the high school where Ruth and I taught for three years, traveled to villages every other weekend to put on a program of music, drama, instruction, and preaching. Today we were taking part in a Big Sunday, where believers from several villages joined together in celebration and in baptizing new converts into the church. Often 1,000 to 3,000 people would attend over a period of several days.

Normally I would have been excited by the prospect, but a lot of things had conspired to deaden my spirits. I had not slept well. It was hot, with temperatures around 100 degrees. The dust, end-of-the-quarter grading, corrections, teachers' meetings—all these were gnawing at me. The rehearsal of our drama the day before had been a disaster. Ruth and I had disagreed over some minor problem. I was not looking forward to going to this distant village: mosquitoes, dark huts, strange foods, hard beds. I did not want to go.

We had been bouncing along for an hour or so over what are sometimes, in moments of unrestrained optimism, referred to as roads, but which are in reality nothing more than dry riverbeds. A lone woman by the side of the road tried to flag us down. Because I did not want my students to think that I was calloused and unfeeling toward those afoot and because I wanted to demonstrate my Christian compassion, I stopped. She came over to the window, and I told her to hop in the back. A moment later I smelled liquor on her breath. We proceeded. As I glanced in the mirror, I noticed that she was behaving strangely, and the boys in the back were somewhat perturbed. I asked the student in the cab with me, named Famon Fa Wiwili Jolbanga Sekesele, what was going on. He said that she was a prostitute.

I will skip ahead in our story. The afternoon of our arrival 130 people were baptized. Later that evening, under the hissing light of a pressure lantern, we presented our drama of Daniel and the lions' den. I did not sleep well that night either, my ears somehow tuned to a mysterious rustling in the thatched roof.

The next morning I found myself seated at the front of the church, just behind the pulpit. The church was packed. People were sitting on each other in the aisles. The front row was one inch from the pulpit, and interested, intent faces peered in the windows, blocking most of the light and effectively preventing even the tiniest wisp of fresh air from entering. The temperature began to rise; my lungs cried out for air. It was already unbearably stuffy and we had not even begun the service.

Finally it started. Exuberant singing of joyful, locally written songs and testimonies came from those who had just been baptized. My shirt clung to me. A man stood up and spontaneously sang. Drops of perspiration rolled down into my eyes, down my nose. An offering was collected amidst rhythmic clapping and singing. My chair was very uncomfortable. One hour went by. More songs, testimonies, a treasurer's report. Two hours. I put my head between my hands so they would think I was praying, but really I was thinking of taking a hike in the cool air of the Cascade Mountains.

Finally Pastor Bobese began to preach, but in a local dialect that I did not understand. Misery. Three hours. Three and a half. Then he gave an invitation to all who wanted Jesus as Lord and Savior. I thought to myself that nobody could possibly have heard any life-changing word in these horrendous circumstances. I even found myself wishing that nobody would respond so we could leave even sooner. Surely all anyone there wanted was simply to escape and breathe fresh air. Anyone who might have been touched by the Word of God could not have budged an inch toward the front. There was no aisle; indeed, there was no front! I then thought of Jesus at Capernaum (Mark 2). The men who really wanted to get to Jesus could not because of the crowd: "There was no room even at the door." I was sure that as Jesus spoke the Word to that crowd, they were no further than one inch away.

Then a woman struggled to her feet crying, gathered up her long skirt, and resolutely began making her way toward the pulpit. People somehow made room for her. Then there was another, and a third, and a fourth; a whole group near the back made their way forward. More and more got up; people left their perches in the windows and came. Came where? Well, behind the pulpit where I was sitting. But as more came, the front "row" moved back into the vacuum, leaving more and more room. I was suddenly surrounded by people of all kinds: old, young, naked, well dressed, men and women—crying, repentant people who wanted to receive Jesus. For several days they had listened to songs, heard testimonies, seen their friends baptized, heard the Word preached and even enacted by our own drama. Now they had decided.

As they pressed around me, what little air I had was gone, but something fresher and more vital poured into my suffocating soul. At first it was sharp and hard, cutting into me, hammering me. I was the one who had hardened myself against the Word. I was the one more concerned with the things of the world: rehearsal, grading, roads, prostitutes, breathing fresh air, and sitting in comfortable chairs. All these people endured these same things and even much more than I. Yet they heard God's Word to them. To me it was as Jeremiah said, "Is not my word like fire . . . and like a hammer which breaks the rock in pieces?" (23:29). It was devastating to me to have the Word strike a hammerblow on my rocklike heart. The Word of God is indeed living and active and sharper than any two-edged sword, piercing as far as the division of soul and spirit, of both joints and marrow, and able to judge the thoughts and intentions of *my* heart.

I was having difficulty controlling my emotions, being so besieged by these people and so pierced by God. Then Pastor Bobese turned and asked me to pray. Pray? Pray!? Feeling the way I did? I stood uncertainly to my feet. From my vantage point of six feet, five inches I noticed the prostitute to whom we had given a ride. She was there, in front, with those who had just come to Jesus. My eyes locked on her. How could I pray? She was the final blow, the irresistible proof and condemnation of my calloused indifference. I knew I had to pray, so I started only to choke up. I could not go on.

There I stood, crying because my sinfulness was so sharply contrasted with God's love. I had taken my proper place as a repentant sinner among the people I had come to serve. Silently I prayed for forgiveness and Jesus—who sympathizes with our weakness because he has been tempted in all things as we, yet without sin—forgave.

All this time, everyone had been waiting patiently for me to continue. Finally, I asked Pastor Bobese to pray in my stead. While he prayed—needing as we did God's forgiveness, cleansing, and redemption, and pierced as we were by the sword of the Spirit which is the Word of God—all of us drew near with confidence to the throne of grace and received mercy and found grace to help in our time of need.

TWENTY-THREE
THE GREAT
BANK ROBBERY

She was weeping for her goods. In the midst of the milling mob, she had simply sat down, her little bundle of currency wrapped in a multicolored scarf folded neatly beside her. Nobody would steal it. What would be the point? The old bills would never be changed into new now. Elbows on knees, she lay her head in her hands. Her thoughts turned to the past few days. Only last week, hadn't she struggled to bring her coffee harvest to market? And now a year's labor lost. The endless days in blurred succession of working in hope, pruning, and weeding the crop, for what? The back bent under 100-pound sacks, neck muscles straining and sweating, a labor driven by hope and now she felt her hope was mauled and tossed aside by the bank. The bank was robbing her. She had heard the manager announce, "The money's all gone," and had heard the gate's iron incisors grind shut.

The stream of murmuring voices from the edges of the crowd filed into the chute of cascading noise as the message was passed on. The bank had closed its doors. The new money was gone, and so then was the old.

Another missionary and I stood in their midst and wondered that a riot did not erupt on the spot. But people were amazingly placid. Perhaps it was the armed soldiers guarding the door that banked the glowing embers of riot. A sense of resignation weighed heavily upon the crowd. Some sat down, others sought to move forward. Few departed, no doubt because they could not believe that this announcement was really the end. In Africa there is always another announcement. The announcement of the money exchange, designed to oust counterfeiters and tighten the money supply had come over the radio, "All citizens and enterprises have three days to change all their bills for new ones. After that, money will be exchanged for half price for one week, then it will not be exchanged at all."

Well, everybody listens to the radio with skepticism. We have heard announcements that Idi Amin was going to drop an atomic bomb on our village and that Queen Elizabeth was about to land in a bush village near us. But soon streams of people were coming to our door. "Did you hear it? Are you going to the bank? Will you take our money?" Pressure built. We had to go. What if it was true? We could not afford to be wrong. So another missionary and I collected all the church, mission, and personal funds we had and set out for the bank on my Yamaha.

Throughout the day we stood without the walls of this financial fortress and within the ranks of the besieging soldiers and people. Each carried a cloth or bag of money. Each kept his or her eyes fixed on the door. Occasionally it would open for some mysterious reason and they would surge towards it. Then the soldiers, concerned with their own safety as much as with the bank's, pushed the front line back.

The course of our spirits began to set with the sun. The sun's heat had wilted us and the bank's searing announcement had withered us. We prepared to leave. Next to us a well-dressed businessman put out his arm. "Wait," he said, "it's not over yet. This is just a ploy to remove those with little money; wait, and the door will be opened for us." I wondered if he knew he was quoting a verse.

The door opened a crack, and heads all looked up in unison. The folded-up woman grabbed her scarf and stood up. The talk tamed to a whisper. A huge man stuck his head timidly out of the door. His beckoning arms waved in the front few people. The rising tide of desperation behind us washed us forward and into the bank. The clanging iron gate shut. The guards forced the people back. There would be no more exchanges for them, ever. We were in, they were out. We learned later that the planeload of new bills coming from Paris was "diverted" by the enemies of the state. Their hopes to create some havoc were realized.

We sorted our money and began to count it in the presence of a clerk. It was dusk in the bank, and the power had failed again. We realized that if we did not finish by dark, they would force us to leave. In the dark it is both impossible to count money and entirely possible to steal it. As we raced against the sun, we saw that another race was developing against supply and demand. There were not enough funds left to change all the money of all the people inside the bank. We counted quickly against both sun and humans, and by God's grace and my missionary friend's previous experience as a teller, we won. The bank's doors were opened once more to let us out. There would be no more exchange at any rate. The despairing woman put her worthless bundle of bills on her head and started home. The confident businessman left carrying no more wealth than the villager next to him. A tremendous leveling process had taken place. Sure, the wealthy would rise again, and the industrious planter would still prosper. However, for that time and place, all the odometers of financial success had been reset to zero.

The African Church lost everything. The coffers in the churches far from any bank became empty. Thieves broke in to steal and they did not even know it. The conference treasuries were eaten by moth and the central account was corrupted by rust. A voice on the radio had pulled the plug on our simple reserves of money.

But the Church awoke the next morning to find it was still the Church. There were no funds to pay the preachers, but they preached. No money to pay the teachers, but they taught. No money to pay their superintendents, but they superintended. The secretaries continued to work and the president led, all without prospects of immediate pay. Certainly they grumbled; stomachs growled and clothes got dirty. But the Church in its mission hardly faltered. More people than ever came to the services, and more people than ever came to the Lord.

TWENTY-FOUR
SACRAMENTAL ELEMENTS AND SACRAMENTAL LIVES

I t was early Sunday morning in a remote village called Kainga. The sun had come up about an hour before and a rooster an hour before that. We had risen, washed, and stumbled, still sleepy-eyed, from the dark hut into the sunlight. Once we had seated ourselves in the low-slung easy chairs, we were handed a cup of overly sweetened, very strong tea. We watched the misty steam rise above the jungle to the accompanying medley of singing birds and beating drums.

As we sat sipping our tea we paused now and then to greet one of the villagers who happened by. "You're up?" they would ask. "Yes, I'm up." "Slept well?" "Yes, well, thank you." You know how those early morning conversations go.

It was a pleasant scene. We wistfully watched babies being washed in large pans and women busy binding up their hair into long spirals. Fires were crackling here and there, boiling water, cooking food; the warmth of the rising sun was bringing the village to life. We were wistful because this was to be our last day in the village after a delightful week's stay.

The village pastor came over to us and we exchanged the usual pleasantries. He looked thoughtful for a moment, then said, "We will have communion during church service this morning." We all agreed that a communion service was a suitable end to our stay. It would testify to the oneness and unity that Christ Jesus had wrought in us. It was impressed on us that in Christ there could be neither Jew nor Greek, male nor female, educated nor illiterate, missionary nor national. And it was, after all, because of that very death and resurrection of which the Lord's Supper speaks that we were there in the first place.

"But" we thought, "they don't have broken bits of crunchy crackers, unsweetened Welch's grape juice, or plastic cups. Certainly they would not think of using a linen-draped communion table. There was not even a book of worship. How would it work?''

After enjoying a breakfast of tea and fried bananas, the pastor beat the drums, calling the Christians to worship. There was no hurry, for there would be two more drums before the service actually began. Then, just after the third drum, one of the deacons approached us. We chatted for a few minutes before he said, ''I wonder what we can use for a white tablecloth for communion.'' We could not think of anything offhand, and he began to look rather dejected. Then Ruth, in a flash of brilliance, thought of our bedsheet and offered that. He was delighted and went back with what he obviously had come for in the first place but had been too polite to ask.

We entered the small mud church with its thatched roof and sat somewhere in the middle on split logs with the rounded side up. The benches might be uncomfortable but they had two advantages: first, they would not rock back and forth, and second, they made it impossible for one to fall asleep. Right away we noticed our long bedsheet gracefully covering the table. The mound on top of the table was immensely large and long. What could be underneath? A curious goat was busy trying to discover the same thing.

After much singing and a short sermon, the communion service began. The pastor pulled back the sheet and folded it with reverence. The mysterious mound was exposed. On the table were dozens of cups and mugs; each communicant had brought his or her own and placed it on the table. There was also a large bowl of cooked and chopped manioc root and a huge pot of tea. The pastor took the bowl of manioc and said, ''The Lord Jesus on the night be was betrayed took bread, and when he had given thanks he broke it and said, 'This is my body which is broken for you; do this in remembrance of me.' '' The bowl was passed and we all took a hefty hunk of manioc and munched it together.

Next he took the pot of tea and said, ''In the same way, after supper he took the cup saying, 'This cup is the new covenant in my blood; do this whenever you drink it in remembrance of me.' '' He then poured a copious amount of tea into each cup and the deacons passed them out. To our surprise, the cups we held were our own, the very ones we had brought with us! After we had drunk together he said, ''Friends, whenever you eat this bread and drink this cup, you proclaim the Lord's death until he comes.''

This last statement had more than passing significance. I was aware that proclamation is what the new Christians did that day and each day. The spectators watching from the windows of the church saw their cousins and uncles, brothers, daughters, and parents testify to their participation in Christ. In a tightly knit village two days' journey into the jungle, one's claims to transformation are easily tested.

The next day we left, but the memory of that Lord's Supper remains with us. Its power was not in its novelty but in sacramental lives that evidenced what the elements symbolize.

TWENTY-FIVE
DOLO'S STORY

I had some aspirin for Dolo's mother, but I wanted to see her before I dispensed it. This strong young man reminded me of a gentle ox. Although he was soft-spoken and polite, his muscles threatened to tear out the seams of his shirt like The Incredible Hulk. I winced at the casual power of his handshake. I had baptized Dolo three years before when he had been among the first four people ever baptized in the remote village along the Dua River. Since then, he had suffered calamitous blows. I had the impression that though his sufferings brought tears to his eyes, no calamity could sway him from the path he had chosen. He had moved along slowly and steadily in his faith.

We entered one room of a large mud hut. The smoke from a fire warmed his mother, who was curled up on a hard reed bed. I bent over to examine her. It was quickly evident that she needed more than aspirin. Admittedly the poverty of my medical knowledge is matched only by my ignorance of nuclear fission, but it seemed obvious that her chest had been broken in some way.

"How did this happen, Dolo?"

"My mother-in-law's family did this to her." He tended to give straightforward answers, Dolo answered questions with a leanness of verbiage bordering on famine. Through a determined inquiry, this story unfolded.

Dolo's wife of twelve years and mother of four living children did not return from the garden one day. After some time, he finally found her barely alive under a fallen tree. As he tells the story, he threw the tree off her like a twig and carried her back to the village. The nurse at the small government dispensary sutured her wounds and tried to straighten out her bones, but the blood loss of the compound fractures of her leg and arm proved fatal. By evening she was dead.

"How does this relate to your injured mother?" I pursued.

He went on. As was their custom, his family carried his wife's body to her natal village, about a day's walk. The maternal side of the family expressed their depth of grief by beating Dolo's mother senseless. As custom dictated, Dolo was forced to stand by and watch. If he intervened, his fate would have been in their hands. As he carried his wife to the village, he had to carry his mother out. Later, his sister was also beaten and returned to her village bed for a month to recover. In one coup, his maternal in-laws eliminated his children's remaining caretakers for an indefinite period. But then the church began to pick up the slack and provided care for the children.

"It is over now that they've vented their grief?"

No, it wasn't. They also "fined" him the equivalent of thirty dollars. In addition, he would have to supply them with a rifle, pots and pans, a mosquito net ("Along the river," said Dolo, "you might have lots of things, but if you don't have a mosquito net, you ain't got nothing."), goats, and a new boat. This in some measure represented what the daughter's death cost the family.

"After they wash me," said Dolo, "then I can find another wife."

The whole process is concluded with a purification ceremony. The in-laws strip him to his underwear and march him down to the river's edge and wash him. When this is done, he is free to find another wife.

"Pastor, as a Christian, should I do all this?" he asked me. Why should he do all this, indeed? He does it for the same reason any of us conform to social expectations. To do otherwise would be to disrupt harmony and invite repercussions ranging from ostracism to murder. No other family would allow their daughter to marry him until he had been cleansed and released.

My first reaction to the question was to shout "NO!" What does a son of the light have to do with darkness? The Christian way is neither to beat and fine and compound grief nor to conform to those who do such.

Being a man who pondered his own words before they left his lips, Dolo waited while I struggled through his question.

On the other hand, as a nonbeliever he had married into the clan and was expected to uphold its implicit social contracts. It was a mechanism designed to facilitate an exchange of goods. It insured that death not be taken cavalierly. Becoming a Christian did not negate his tribal obligations. Should he refuse, it would only become an opportunity to shame the Christian community for their bad citizenship.

He sat for a long time after I offered this comment. Finally he said, "My next wife will come from a Christian family."

PART EIGHT
AMERICAN TOURISTER

We may have left Africa,
but Africa never really left us.

PERSPECTIVE

Just when you think you have set your wheels on the inside track, just when you begin to whisper, "I think I understand," something happens that seems perfectly ordinary to everyone but you. The Event, when it happens, blows over your straw house with one wolf-puff. Your hypotheses and assumptions lie in ruins. You say to yourself, "There is no such thing as a veteran missionary, only an older one."

Try as we might to travel light and "live off the land," we are forever visitors for the simple reason that whenever we wish we can leave. Just leave. The ability to wave farewell and slam shut the airplane door makes us different. It gives us a daring freedom to risk, because we can, after all, escape. No matter how hard it gets, we know our Year of Jubilee, i.e., furlough, looms ahead.

I leave for every furlough convinced I am incurably American and arrive stateside feeling more than half African, no longer in step with any culture, sharing a similar worldview with no one except a few other missionaries. Never acculturated, the missionary becomes bicultural, perhaps happiest in the air, jetting from one land to another. "Since we live on the borderline between different worlds, we find that no matter where we are, we are not quite at home. We are never fully assimilated into our second culture, but after a while we no longer fit our first culture either, because we have been changed and influenced by our experiences."[1]

Sooner or later, when our friends are less intrigued with our "exotic" life and the church has seen our slides, they will inevitably ask, "When are you going back?" When are we going back, indeed? At first we are overjoyed to be in North America again. We revel in the convenience and wallow in the comfort. But it is not long before one of our children also wistfully asks, "When can we go back, Daddy?" Then our thoughts turn to Luyada, Mbangiye, Saki, Tobogo, and the warmth and joy and acceptance that have surrounded us. We realize that we may have left Africa, but Africa had never really left us.

[1] Paul Hiebert, *Anthropological Insights for Missionaries* (Grand Rapids, MI: Baker Book House, 1985), p. 238.

TWENTY-SIX
GO WELL, WHITE MAN

I was ambling across the hospital grounds one night about ten o'clock, minding my own business. I have since learned to always appear in a hurry. One of our doctors materialized out of the night and stood before me. With studied nonchalance he asked me if I would go on a dead run that night. The request was made with all the emotion of Attila the Hun dispatching an enemy. Since then I have also learned to keep a ready-made list of excuses handy. But for the moment I was empty-handed, so I agreed.

The good doctor walked me over to the hospital truck, which was surrounded by a group of grieving people. He pointed at the motionless form covered with a sheet in the back. I knew what it was; he didn't have to tell me.

"That's a body," he said, oblivious to my keen perception. "The fellow died here about an hour ago. His family wants to take him back to Bolupulu tonight."

I also correctly anticipated the next move.

"Here's the keys. Bye, and thanks." Off he went, probably to play Rook.

I jangled the keys in my hand and tried to size up the situation. The sliver of a moon revealed just enough to make me a believer, if I had not been already. The eerie death-wail attacked my nerves like agent orange.

"Let's go!" I decreed, and in they got and off we went.

The violent expression of grief continued for about three minutes; then it stopped. In its place rose a low murmur of voices and, yes, laughter leaked into my cab. Finally, I rolled down the windows. The mourning had ceased at the edge of the mission compound. It was now resembling an apres-funeral coffee klatsch. Well, at least it would make a more pleasant trip.

Without warning I jammed on the brakes, neatly stacking my passengers one on top of another behind my window. Eyes and teeth greeted me in the rearview mirror. A soldier had stepped out onto the road. As a courtesy, I always stop for armed soldiers in the middle of the road.

"You going to Bolupulu?" he asked.

Briefly I flirted with which answer would be more advantageous. News travels faster than a hot-footed centipede in Africa, so I decided to tell the truth.

"Yes."

"Well, when you are done there, go on to Jekube and pick up a man there. Bring him back. He killed his wife."

I had opted for the wrong answer after all. But, as with the doctor, I detected no undue note of excitement in his voice. He could have been asking me for the time. Certainly this murderer was in custody. They must be looking for a way to bring him back. The police in Africa are often short of vehicles and to assist them is not unusual. "Better to volunteer than to be commandeered" is an old missionary adage.

I knew we were nearing Bolupulu because the mournful wail sputtered again into combustion in the back of the pickup. The crying was also a signal to the villagers that they were returning with bad news. The truck rolled through the village and created a wake of people behind it as they ran into the road to join the dirge. Someone banged loudly on the cab roof—the traditional signal to stop.

The corpse was unloaded. I watched the scene unfold before me. The people threw themselves on the ground. They tossed dirt into the air while others rent their clothes. My rear emergency blinkers were intermittently flashing off and on, creating a stop action drama bathed in red. I had been to several Christian wakes before this. Never had I beheld such an acting out of grief.

My task was done, yet another remained. Where was Jekube? I did not know for sure. I gunned the hearse past one village and another. No sign of a murderer anywhere, and I was not about to go door to door.

Then, up ahead a light arched back and forth across the road. It had to be the police flagging down an unsuspecting truck. Wouldn't they be surprised when I told them I had just changed my sign on the windscreen from hearse to paddy wagon. I coasted to a stop near the man. He stuck his head in the window and smiled. I smiled back.

"Hello, I killed my wife and we need a ride back to town."

Whatsamatter Hill, cat got your tongue? No one else in sight, just him and me. He looked friendly enough. Maybe her death was just an accident. In any case, I was going to pretend it was.

"O.K. Hop in . . . the back."

"Just a minute."

Off he trotted around the corner. Then he came back carrying something distressingly familiar across his shoulders. I knew what it was; he didn't have to tell me. Déjà vu.

"This is my wife," he said and climbed into the back.

There was only one thing to do—take him directly to jail and do not pass Go. I successfully forced the questions out of my mind during the trip back. Was he expecting me? Why didn't he try to flee the police? Why is everybody so matter-of-fact about a slaying? Why didn't the police come with me? Since I had no intention of interviewing either the gendarme or the passenger, I would never know for sure. I speculated that he couldn't just run to another village and hide; everybody would know him immediately. And then again the judicial system had so many holes in it that it only stayed afloat by plugging them with currency.

Bang! Bang! Bang! My reverie was reverberated out of my head by his signal to stop.

"Here's the jail!" he shouted.

He jumped out, then reached in for his stiffening bundle. With a grunt he hauled her onto his shoulders.

"Thanks for the ride," he said by the window.

"Don't mention it," I responded.

"Go well, white man."

TWENTY-SEVEN
EXCESS BAGGAGE

He kneed him viciously in the groin. Then as the man convulsed in agony, he brought up a double clenched fist in a powerful uppercut. The now helpless victim sprawled backward and fell. His opponent sprang high into the air, landing squarely on his chest with both boots. Rolling from side to side and holding his apparently splintered ribs, the wreckage of a man was defenseless. But his pursuer was heartlessly unrelenting. Circling around behind like a jackal sensing the kill, he leapt again, this time onto his head. Each boot drove against his skull. Finally he let up. The man was obviously crushed and dying. He turned his back and raised his arms in victory.

Miraculously, the carnage of suffering flesh and broken bones rose again from the dead. Suddenly the strutting victor gasped as his eyes bulged. Ten iron fingers seized his throat. The resurrected corpse ran with the red-faced prey and smashed his skull into a steel post. He slumped unconscious to the ground amid our roars of delight.

Professional wrestling had come to Africa via the tube.

Pastor Bangamo and I had arrived at the plantation at suppertime. The expatriate overseer politely asked us to join his family for a meal. A large black-and-white TV dumped its shaded images into the room.

Pastor Bangamo had never seen a TV before, though he knew about them. His first introduction to this marvelous piece of western technology was Gorgeous George. We, of course, having been nurtured at television's friendly breast, grew up with such goings on as sheer entertainment. We understood that the fight was showmanship. Nobody could possibly survive such brutality. We slurped our soup and gurgled with amusement at their obvious antics.

Pastor Bangamo stared transfixed at the screen. Before him was pictured a life-and-death struggle without rules. No holds were barred in this fight between two gargantuan men. Our chuckles were to him wholly inconsistent with the bloodshed he was witnessing. There was no possible way he could assimilate a television in the jungle or its films of mortal hand-to-hand combat with the merry laughter of his missionary colleague. I had just spent the week with him on an evangelism trip. He had never heretofore suspected my underlying blood lust.

Finally, the cognitive dissonance was unbearable. He turned to look at me. Twice he tried to formulate a question, working his lips silently, but the incongruities he was experiencing were a hemorrhage of comprehension. What was the context? What were the questions? What was the meaning? Why? Who? How . . . ?

I explained that they were only acting and it was sheer entertainment. That explanation only made his pain more acute. Why would people play like that? After some discussion, my elucidations began to penetrate. Finally he said, "That belongs to you, not to us."

The guests had brought their own baggage.

TWENTY-EIGHT
RULES OF THE ROAD

In the Book of Missionary Laws and Axioms, you will find Law Number 14b: *You can't get there from here.* Ignorance of this law made our flight home to the United States very difficult. Knowledge of the law doesn't help either, because any change of itinerary only creates new, unobtainable destinations. With care we selected our route out of Africa: direct to Marseilles, then to Paris and Chicago. We ordered our tickets from an agent in the capital. Two weeks to D-Day, plenty of time. We forgot, though, that *it is always too late, no matter when you start.*

We pretended for a week that no news was good news, that our tickets were ready and waiting for us. Then Message Number One came over the radio: "Your route no longer possible, unless you wait eighteen hours in the Tripoli airport for connecting flight." Quadaffy was not noted for welcoming tourists, and so we declined. We discovered an alternate route via Ndgemena and Nice to Paris. With three days to go Message Number Two came back: "Ndgemena airport now in rebel hands; suggest alternate routing." Finally by the help of ULTRA and UNIVAC we found an Aeroflot flight that exited the Southern Hemisphere by way of Khartoum, Cairo, and Beirut, en route to Moscow. The light dimmed and flickered as she suggested another place for us to get off. But since we had friends in Cairo, we finally opted to disembark in Egypt. Two days before departure.

We flew MAF to the capital and asked our host missionaries if there was an Egyptian embassy. They didn't know. Never needed one. Undaunted, we walked out to the main road and flagged a taxi.

"Take us to the Egyptian Embassy," I commanded tersely. We flagged another taxi. And another. Finally one agreed. He gunned the engine and off we sped, apparently to the Egyptian Embassy. A half hour later some of the roads began to look familiar.

"Say, haven't we come by here before, driver?"

"Non, non, Monsieur."

"Do you know where the Egyptian Embassy is?"

"Non, non, Monsieur. I do know where the Sudanese Embassy is, though." And off we went again. We braked in front of the Sudanese flag, and saw next to it a welcome sign, "Egyptian Embassy."

In we walked, full of false confidence. *The person who tries to rush in Africa is easily buried,* yet we needed a visa in order to get the tickets for our flight out the next day. *Act as though you had more time than they—* Hill's missionary axiom, seldom followed.

A sleek and beautiful receptionist greeted us warmly. She heard our request, took our passports and off she whisked saying, "It will just take a minute." We looked at each other in disbelief.

We had just settled down to read an Egyptian publication, or rather look at the pictures, when in she glided again, all smiles.

"That fast?" queried Ruth.

"No, there is, how you say it, a little problem."

"Oh?"

"Yes, you have no more pages to stamp in the visa. If you had room," she shrugged, "you would have them now." She snapped her fingers.

I glanced at my watch. It was 10:30 a.m. At noon the city went into a long hibernation, opening again in the late afternoon.

"When do you open this afternoon?"

"Fifteen hours."

Easy. We could rush to the American Embassy, get new pages, come back for the visa, and still make it to the Aeroflot office before it closed at seventeen hours.

Never say "quickly" to a taxi driver. We ricocheted through the narrow corridors lined with people, sped the wrong way around a round-point resembling the Arc de Triomphe, and we were there. I shakily gave him a tip. We dashed inside and breathlessly asked through the bullet-proof glass where to get visa-extensions for our passports.

"I'm sorry. The vice-consul is not in."

"When will he be back?"

"Sometime this afternoon." We just weren't going to make it.

Everything takes longer than you think, unless you slow down; then it happens before you are ready. We walked slowly back to the guest house. We had several hours to kill. Then we passed the post office with the sign "Communication Internationale." A ghastly thought dawned on us. Our friend in Cairo had not yet been notified that we were coming. We suddenly had a way of filling in the time. Obediently we went in the door under the sign.

"Oui?" said the girl behind the counter. The room was lined with telephone booths, several occupied. It looked like the right place.

"We would like to place a call to Cairo."

She opened a large loose-leaf notebook and searched diligently for something, maybe the code for Cairo. A few minutes later she said, "You will have to make the call over there where they sell stamps, Monsieur, Madame." It was not the right place. *The right place is always over there.*

We trotted over to the other side of the building and posed the same question. The same formidable book appeared, the same process was begun. Finally she look at us and said, "You can't call Cairo until tomorrow afternoon." I supposed the line was busy. Ruth gave her a look that said, "What really is the matter? You can tell me. I'll understand." The girl added, "I am sorry, I don't know how to make the call. Come back tomorrow when another person is on duty."

The expert is never in is a law written on the tombstone of many a missionary. We straggled home, despondent, until Ruth hit upon the perfect solution. Call Mom in the States, and let her call Egypt!

With no trouble we got Mom on the line. She hadn't heard my voice for four years. The trouble was it was 3:00 a.m. in Seattle. Mom isn't at her best until sometime later.

"Hi Mom. It's Brad."

"Wa, who, huh . . . ?"

"Would you call this number in Cairo, Egypt: 321-5768-754, and tell Mr. Bonnet, that's B-O-N-N-E-T, that we will arrive in Cairo about 11:30 p.m. on Aeroflot, A-E-R-O-F-L-O-T, flight number 765?"

The strangled sounds on the other end were costing us plenty. The connection couldn't have been that bad.

"Got that?"

"Uh, yes, uh, Brad—is that you?"

The static was building and we could hardly hear each other. "Yeah, Mom. Call him and tell him. . . ." The line went dead.

"Did she get it?" Ruth asked.

"Most of it." I was hopeful.

At fifteen hours we were at the Embassy doors when they opened. The receptionist led us into the consul's office. He heard our story, and reached into his drawer for a bottle of Elmer's glue. He smirked.

"Bet you thought this would be some complicated procedure?"

Merci. He glued in the pages, and handed them back. We were out the door before he finished saying goodbye. To the Egyptian Embassy we sped once again. We walked into a deserted waiting room. I coughed. No answer. "Hello!" I hailed. Nothing. At sixteen hours a man who was obviously of ambassador status strode in through the front doors. His tailored suit did him justice. His heels clicked over the marble surface. We rose to meet him. After explaining our situation again, he disappeared into his office. A half hour later he came out and handed our visas to us with a flourish. We started for the door.

"There's just one small matter."

We froze. Our hearts stopped.

"When you arrive, you must change $300 each for Egyptian money."

We hadn't $150 between us. Money was waiting for us in Marseilles, where we weren't going. Law: *Never cross a bridge before you get to it.*

We arrived at the Aeroflot office ten minutes before closing. The agent handling our tickets was not in. Explaining that our flight left at 10:00 a.m. the next morning didn't produce him, either.

"Mais, Monsieur, we will bring it to your lodging first thing in the morning." *First thing in the morning is always too late.* His assurances only made me chew my Rolaids more rapidly. *But when all else fails, fall softly and gently into the welcoming arms of resignation.*

I was still dreaming of sheiks and harems of receptionists when an insistent pounding on our door rent my fantasyland. I opened the door in my tropical pajamas, a pair of fruit-of-the-looms, with my tousled hair and beard stubble to greet the immaculately suited travel agent.

"Your tickets, sir," he said. He looked me up and down in barely suppressed disbelief. "You are leaving today?" Appearances are deceiving.

A faint spark of hope flamed into life once again. Now if the plane wasn't overbooked, if it actually left, if Mom had dialed Mr. Bonnet, if we got past the moneychangers . . . we were home free. *The probabilities of success decrease with the appearance of good fortune.*

We boarded the plane without trouble and took our seats directly behind two elderly missionaries that we knew from the field. The Russian plane took off and turned its nose towards Khartoum, site of Gordon's last stand against the Mahdist rising.

A buxom stewardess with red ruby lips and sharp Slavic features made her way down the aisle carrying a tray of glasses, half full of a pale-clear liquid. Evidently there was no option but to take what she offered. She set one down firmly in front of each passenger and moved on. It was unthinkable to refuse. Besides she was probably KGB. When the missionaries in front of us managed to decline, I realized what it was—a moment too late. Ruth had seized her glass of "water" and slogged it back in one mouthful. A look of animal desperation shone in her eyes as she struggled to get her breath. She clutched her throat and panted and would have fallen out into the aisle had I not comfortingly restrained her by clamping my hand over her mouth. Finally, she croaked, "That wasn't water." Again about the appearances.

The saintly white-haired woman in front turned around and said sweetly, "We don't drink vodka." I grinned wickedly back at her. What missionaries loose on furlough won't try!

The stopover at Khartoum was made without incident, though my brief impression was that Gordon should have defended someplace else. The plane touched down in Cairo at exactly midnight. The blast of hot desert air even at that time of night was enough to bake bread. We straggled across the concourse and into the unairconditioned building. At least outside there was a breeze, even if it came from the jet engines. Immediately in front of us loomed the sign: Exchange. In apprehension we approached the fat, sweating man reigning over the little booth.

"Three hundred dollars each," he said without looking up.

"Ah, yes, we'll be right back."

We hadn't lived these years in Africa for nothing. We went and re-trieved our suitcases, allowing a suitable amount of time to pass. Then I marched back to the window and declared in firm resonant terms learned in homiletics, "I want to cash $100." He changed the money, again with-out looking up. *When at a loss never ask questions, give orders.*

We began looking about for some sign of Mr. Bonnet, but as we were still on the wrong side of customs no one was visible. We chose the short-est line filtering past the severe-looking agents. Our line, a half hour later, was the longest. *Never choose the shortest line.* They were checking every article minutely; hat bands, suitcase linings, the inside of lotion bottles. We might well spend our vacation time in line.

A pleasant middle-aged man with a grey mustache sidled up to us. "Are you Americans?"

Another one of those trick questions. It was a useless game to outwit the bearer of such inquiry.

"Yes." We looked it, anyway.

"Ah, yes, well, just follow that green line," he said, pointing to the green line painted on the floor.

What had we to lose? We hefted our luggage and began to follow the path. It wound around lines of passengers and out past a little unat-tended desk, down the hall, past a young, armed guard, and . . . outside!

"Brad, I think we had better go back. We just can't walk out like this."

We retraced our steps back up the green line, past the guard who smiled quizzically at us, then back into the waiting room, where we stood like ostriches on hard pan.

The same man came over again. "Please, you may go out this way!" He pointed out the path to freedom once again.

"Well, what about customs and all that?" I finally had the presence of mind to inquire. I wanted to ask, "And who the heck are you?" but thought it impolitic.

"I am a customs man, yes? You go out that way? No?!" Yes. So out again past the guard we went.

"Going to get a taxi," I said slowly to the guard, pointing at the line of them.

"Sure man, anyone you want," he said. "Don't let 'em take you for more than two pounds, though." He smiled. "University of Chicago, Class of '75."

A cry went up as we emerged from the sanctuary of the building. Still no sign of Mr. Bonnet. But we did have the name of a little hotel he had recommended some months back. We were engulfed with whirl-ing robes and outstretched hands. Each driver was determined to get part of us. I selected one.

"Two pounds, town?" I pointed off into the blackness in what was, I hoped, the general direction of town.

He showed no sign of comprehension.

"Two pounds," I said, holding up two fingers.

He spat and looked at my two wavering fingers. I held up another, to make it three. He got ready to spit again. The clamor wasn't subsiding either, but grew as the bartering continued. I was on the point of holding up one more. I would have eventually held up all the fingers I possessed. He held up six.

Our friend the armed graduate sauntered over. "Having some trouble?"

"Ah, er, no, just can't get them to take us for less than six."

"Six?!" He was genuinely horrified. He pointed to the unfortunate driver and said a few, apparently effective, words. The driver shouted back at him, grabbed our bags, and stuffed them into the trunk. Quickly we darted inside, and away we went into the Arabian night with a howl of rubber and a string of indignant oaths.

We raced off into the blackness towards Hotel Jean. The driver muttered to himself as he went, following no particular line of traffic, honking vigorously all the while.

"Brad, I don't think he is happy with us."

Our thoughts turned gloomy. We might never meet Mr. Bonnet. Years from now they would uncover our remains in the desert. But we did come into the magnificent city of Cairo at about 1:30 a.m. We went past what was obviously the tourist section with the major hotels. Slowly we made our way into what Arthur Fommer calls the "native section." I am sure that Cairo is the only city in the world where you can buy anything you want in the middle of the street at 1:30 in the morning.

The driver nosed his taxi in between two ox carts and stopped. He pointed down a little alley. We strained to see, but could just make out a half-lit sign, "Hotel Jean." There had to be another Hotel Jean! This couldn't possibly be it.

We got out first. Then he got out, opened the trunk, and put our bags on the ground with his foot on top. He held up the number six. Six, six, six, the Beast. I tried to save face by arguing but we knew all along that I would pay up. He shook his head and shouted something at me. A few passersby stopped. We continued the discussion; a small crowd began to gather. Then a sweet feminine voice in a British accent cut through the hubbub.

"May I help you?"

"Yes, we were just paying the taxi driver, and . . ."

She paid him three pounds, said a few things to him; he smiled and even waved to us as he went back to his cab. He held the door open for her. She had hired the taxi herself.

"My husband and I were just going out to the airport to meet some friends of his from Central Africa. We are fortunate to get a cab this time of night. . . . Why, what's the matter?"

Something in our expressions must have alarmed her.

"My goodness, what is it?" Then light dawned on her. "You're the . . . the . . ."

Ruth finished, "the Hills."

Mr. Bonnet just then came up and joined the laughing group. He had gotten all the information—except the time was wrong. Miracle of miracles, we met.

I let Mr. Bonnet dismiss the taxi driver. Last law: *Missionaries' mothers do it right.*

TWENTY-NINE
REENTRY

We could see them waving frantically from the overhead viewing platform. It would have been embarrassing except that everybody was doing it. Sufficient numbers make any behavior acceptable. We waved back. I hoisted a featureless little bundle of blankets into the air for the grandparents to see, a trophy beyond ivory tusks from our term in Zaire. They clapped with glee and pointed at the pink bundle covering their yet unseen granddaughter.

The rivulets of SAS passengers backed up behind the customs desks. Every country has its own queuing traditions, and the traveler who has not learned them is always the last one through. Families with children may board first; however, they disembark last. Despite our acquired African aggression at the gates, we found ourselves at the back of the group and an hour from those wet grandma kisses and awkward grandpa hugs.

The heated emotions of reentering the American atmosphere were threatening to burn off our protective tiles. We imaged ourselves one or two steps out of cultural sync: I still wearing a leisure suit and Ruth's dresses inches too low, or too high. We didn't know the top ten, or the current TV rages. All the media that form an implicit base of communication commonality seemed to be lacking.

I still remembered vividly our last reentry burnout. It was occasioned by the society at large: consumptive, casual, calloused, permeated by blatant strivings and watching out for Number One, characterized by a splintering individualism that so defies the black spirit. It was occasioned by sensory overload: neon lights, advertising, noise, sales pitches, billboard sex, and an array of choice in every domain that challenges one to order a hamburger—much less select a dress or buy a car. Our systems were heated by churches and friends that, in all good faith and the best of interests, treated us like returning conquerors rather than the occasionally successful failures we felt ourselves to be. Or they regarded us as oddities to be tolerated; there's one in every family.

But this time we were, we hoped, more experienced cultural astronauts. We could more easily change orbits and vehicles of expression.

Rachel pointed up at the eager faces. "Who are all those people?"

"Those are your grandmas and grandpas."

"And over there?"

Uncles and aunts.

Nephews and cousins.

Pastor, friends.

The titles mystified her, but we had had many long talks about "them." She knew they were somehow family and cared for her. They were the ones who sent presents and cards.

"We cannot meet them yet. We have to pass through customs first." Truer than words.

She started to scamper ahead, oblivious to our commands to come back. Finally Ruth's sharp command in Lingala, "Jila awa!" brought her to a halt.

Suddenly a man grinning from ear to ear appeared at our side.

"Hi! I'm Bud McBride." He introduced himself. "You're the Hills, I know. Here, I'll take you through customs." I gathered by his badge, impressive key ring, and beeper that he was a VIP customs agent. But I had learned to be wary of overfriendly customs agents.

"Follow me!"

We didn't move. He looked behind at us, then came back, smiling. "I'm Bud McBride," he said again. "You know, from church!"

Light dawned. I remembered now that one of the newer church members was a customs agent. In fact, most of the membership roll was different; no doubt so were their customs.

"We'll get you through customs in no time." He led us through the crowd to a little gate on the other side that he opened with a key. The agent on duty raised an inquisitive eyebrow.

"Missionaries from Africa," said Bud, explaining everything.

The agent grunted, not as impressed as I had hoped. He pointed to our largest suitcase. A very nonverbal sort, evidently. I reached for the suitcase keys I had been carrying like a talisman for days just for this occasion. I blanched, then groped hopelessly in my other pocket. As people do under duress, I searched the same pockets again and again in disbelief. A scene from Orwell's 1984 choked me up: Winston's worst fears were discovered by his tormentors, and orchestrated to drive him beyond terror. My secret phobia was losing my keys during a customs inspection. Now it was happening!

"Where did you put the keys, Ruth?" I said, stalling for time.

"You didn't, you didn't? You did?" Perfect meter. She didn't answer my question.

"Hmmmmm," said the agent.

"What's in the suitcase?" asked Bud.

"Clothes."

"Is that all?"

"No, some books, pictures."

"Nothing to declare?"

That is a trick question. I've learned the trick answer.

"Like what, for instance?"

"Whiskey, cigarettes, perfume, fruit. . . ."

"No, none of that."

"Nothing else?"

I smiled as if making a joke. "Just ivory, poison arrows, kisolo beans, a python skin, and a spearhead." They all laughed at my attempt at humor.

"Go on through."

But it had been no joke.

We were through! Just steps away were the big swinging doors that led outside to the wide open spaces of the U.S.A.—to the unfamiliar, to friends, and to family. We stood there behind the doors for a long moment, close together. McBride must have sensed what we were feeling, and stood unobtrusively behind us. Ruth secured her grip on the infant. I took Rachel's hand. We caught occasional penny-arcade glimpses of our family, frozen in various postures as the doors swung to and fro.

I took a deep breath. "Here we go." We walked through the last doors.

"There they are!" squealed a familiar voice. The we were absorbed into the enveloping warmth of love.

"Let me see that precious little bundle!"

"How are you, Rachel? I'm Cousin Brenda!"

"When are you going back?" The dreaded question.

"How's Africa?" Different. . . .

"Good flight?" Yes, except for the detour through Khartoum and Cairo.

"Here, let me take that suitcase. What's in it anyway?"

"We missed you." And we you.

"Bless the Lord!" said a grandpa voice. O my soul, all that is within me, bless his holy name.

EPILOGUE

CHRISTIAN FOXHOLES: FINDING MYSELF IN LUKE 9:57-62

In a society inundated with advertisements and slogans, evangelicals have not been left out. We have "I'm born again" bumper stickers and "I'm born again" T-shirts. Born-again believers unite for political action and charitable causes. "Born again" has become a catchword in its own right. When Ronald Reagan was asked if he was born again, he answered in good African fashion, "How am I not born again?" Billy Carter once remarked that there are more beer drinkers than born-again Baptists.

The meaning of the term "born again" has been cheapened. The new birth has come to mean something less than responding to Jesus' call to discipleship, "Follow me." Apparently we can be born again without dying first; we can have Jesus in our hearts without having Jesus in our hearts. One is not born again into never-never-land; one is born again into discipleship—and often by discipleship.

Jesus used the phrase "born again" only with Nicodemus, who suffered great agony of decision. A year later he was still equivocating, citing Mosaic law in a feeble attempt to protect Jesus but not follow him. It was no easy decision for Nicodemus to bury Jesus and risk expulsion from the synagogue. More often Jesus asked people to follow him unconditionally, to sell all and take up the cross.

The new birth is preceded by a hard time of counting the cost of discipleship, of evaluating, sifting, and painful decision-making. If this term is shortened or bypassed, we have premature birth into the family of God. Because the process of counting the cost is cut short, many are born weak, shrinking from even minimal kingdom requirements. Often this natural process of cost-counting is weakened by listening to the relaxants of religious platitudes and consuming a fiberless diet of God's promises without his requirements.

The importance of the due process of birth was brought home to me one night in a remote village along the Dua River. After I had preached that evening, I sat down. The audience encircling me was supposed to disperse and go home. The service was over. I had said the amen. Bye, everybody. But they didn't leave. The noise level increased. Maybe they didn't understand. So I stood up again and said loudly in my best dialect, "The service is finished." The official pronouncement had all the effect of a placard at a convention. They still ringed us.

So I sat down again. Pastor Mbangiye sat next to me completely unperturbed. But then he is always unperturbed. He is a former elephant hunter, and not too many elephant hunters retire. The other missionary on my right was looking for a bolt hole if things got out of hand. I followed his eyes, thinking I might follow right after him. The fact that we were two days journey from "civilization" (i.e., soft beds, American foods, and English language) in a village that had not invited us, did not add to any sense of sublime peace as we sat there. Neither did the jungle noises nor the long shadows cast by a full moon.

Then a man with the physique of Arnold Schwarzenegger stepped before us. He deliberately seemed to move so that the yellow moonlight illuminated him as fully as possible. He crossed his arms and stood in silent contemplation before us. The crowd grew so quiet you could hear a hippo snort. He had our undivided attention. Finally he spoke.

"Why is it you Protestants call our medicine sin? I make medicine to help people, not to hurt them. I help people who go mad. I can cure them. If I become a Christian, do I have to give this up?"

I started to formulate a clear, concise answer. I said, "Well, I, er, that is, I mean to say. . . ."

Then Pastor Mbangiye rose to his feet and answered him. "There are two kinds of medicine, one natural involving herbs, the other diabolic, using spirits. The former we accept, the latter God hates." The man, satisfied, moved back into the circle.

Another man stepped into the center. He explained that he had been baptized Catholic as an infant, as had most of the villagers. If he became Protestant, would he have to be rebaptized? How does Protestant baptism differ from Catholic? I quickly reviewed a half dozen books I've read on baptism and the Anabaptists. Sacrosanct terms like as "prevenient grace" and "baptismal regeneration" raced through my mind. How could I say "divine ordinance" in dialect? Before I could organize it all into coherent language, Pastor Mbangiye again got up and explained that we didn't want him to abandon Catholicism to become Protestant, we wanted him to abandon himself to Christ first. The man was taken aback.

One after another, individuals came forward with questions. "If we are saved by faith as you say, what exactly is wrong with drinking?" "The pope is our head, and you are therefore religious rebels. Explain." "We don't worship Mary and the saints, but they are our advocates. What is wrong with that?" "Why is the Protestant Bible different than the Catholic version?"

I was relieved when this evangelistic college-bowl broke up. Whatever happened to the simple, ignorant native, the kind that would trade Manhattan Island for a few beads? We realized that we had not come with a brand-new message but with a new interpretation of a message they had already heard. We came proclaiming rebirth into eternal life by God's grace and our response in faith. We could not preach in a vacuum. They had to test our message with their questions and examine the good news in the arena of their lives. They were counting the cost, not willing to commit themselves to following Jesus until they were sure they understood the basic requirements of discipleship.

In the encounters summarized for us in Luke 9:57-62, Jesus lays down three obstacles for discipleship and three commands for following him.

The first obstacle is our reluctance to part with that sense of security found in property and ownership. The command is, "Count the cost!" In this passage, the first man is a volunteer. To volunteer is a North American tradition of heroism. Often a volunteer perceives a particular personal advantage. More often the volunteer has not anticipated the real cost. He or she has not read the fine print. But in Luke 9:57 we have an eager volunteer. He declares to Jesus, "I will follow you wherever you go." Jesus replies, "Foxes have holes and birds of the air have nests; but the Son of man has nowhere to lay his head" (v. 58). Jesus did not encourage him. Instead he repelled him. He did not lay out the benefits the volunteer would have but talked of suffering and deprivation. How many men would volunteer for the Marine Corps if bullet-riddled bodies and legless veterans were advertised instead of world cruises and medical care? A few good recruits would soon become no recruits at all. Jesus does not propose a following of easy belief, or a born-again experience with general anesthesia. When preaching the Gospel, how easy it is to list the advantages of "signing up with Jesus": free ticket to heaven, showers of blessings, terrific fellowship, answered prayer, parking spots in front, prompt healings, and free coffee after church.

At a recent Bible camp I overheard a counselor persuading her high-school charges to become Christians. "It's really simple; nothing to it. Just say 'Jesus, I invite you into my heart.' It's easy, try it." It sounded like a Jesus commercial on TV. Try it, you'll like it. If you don't, you can get a refund.

There is no formula to recite to become a Christian, no easy mantra. The mere words "I invite you into my heart" are easy, but the commitment necessary to make those words meaningful requires a long, hard term of labor.

Foxholes are a temporary refuge at best. The fox lives outside, not inside. The image reminds me of a cartoon I once saw. Two disheveled soldiers were snug and smug in a little foxhole. They couldn't see out, but huge tanks were closing in on them from every side. One was saying to another, "We should dig it deeper." Neither deeper holes nor increased financial security guarantee salvation.

Jesus was concerned that this overeager volunteer slow down and evaluate more deeply. Jesus caused him to search, and, it is hoped, in the end to form a greater attachment to himself. He underscores that there is no real security in property or ownership. The first obstacle to following him is the reluctance to part with that sense of security found in our investments. The first command therefore is "Count the cost!" Ours is a costly faith.

The second obstacle to following Jesus is our bondage to seemingly insurmountable circumstances. The corresponding command is, "Be ready now!"

The second person mentioned is not a volunteer but a conscript. Jesus gives him a lengthy speech of "Follow me!" But he replies, "Lord, let me first go and bury my father." He is willing to go, but not immediately, not on Jesus' terms. This is an enigmatic passage that could mean one of three things. His father might already have been dead and needed only a proper burial. Or perhaps the father was terminally ill and would die soon. Or yet again, his statement could have been an idiomatic expression meaning he must discharge his family duties until that time when he could reasonably be free of them. In any case, Jesus' intent is clear; he says, in effect, "Friend, there will never be a time when all your circumstances are just right, when everything falls into place to permit you to follow me. Trust me for your family; you go and proclaim the kingdom of God. It is near, for I am here." We must act when the Spirit speaks.

A fellow once said, "Opportunity knocked on my door today, but by the time I unlocked three locks, unhooked the chain, turned off the burglar alarm, and leashed the doberman, it was gone." Just as today is the day of salvation, now is the moment to move out and follow Jesus.

One evening I was driving through Chicago, down Michigan Avenue. Before me stretched a dozen lights, some red and some green. If I had waited until they were all green, I would never have moved. When the first one flashes green, a person is to move ahead until stopped by the next red. By the time all the lights in your life are green and permit you to follow, somebody may be waiting to bury you and you will have missed the opportunity.

Note that as with the first man, Jesus offers no assurances. He does not say, "Follow me and everything will be fine; your father will not die." Our discipleship does not insure us or our family from calamity, death, or hardship.

The first obstacle is our reluctance to part with our foxholes; the first command is "Count the cost." The second obstacle is our bondage to seemingly insurmountable circumstances: debts to pay, family to care for, prior engagements. The second command to follow is, "Be ready now." To be clear, Jesus is not advocating irresponsibility either, like the born-again businessperson who insisted that *all* his old debts had been cancelled. What Jesus wants is our "Yes! Here I come, ready or not," our naked leap from the boat into the sea. Leave the circumstances for Jesus to work out around you and through you.

The Lord works in a unique fashion in every life. Once Ruth and I made the commitment to follow Jesus wherever he led, I was promoted from busboy to floor captain of a restaurant. That brought in enough income to live on. The Lord led us into an experimental program at Seattle Pacific University and through it provided our entire senior-year tuition, permitting us to finish our preparation for the field. At the last minute, Ruth was a credit short for graduation, but it was waived so we left on schedule. But the commitment to go was a leap by faith and not by sight. We believed there was a net, but we would not see it until we landed.

The third obstacle to following Jesus is our emotional dependency on all that is familiar. The challenging command of Jesus is, "Follow with an undivided heart."

The third person in the text is a volunteer but differs from the first in setting certain conditions. He volunteers service but says, "First let me go back and say goodbye to my family."

A study of missionaries concluded that there was no common denominator or personality trait among them and the most successful were those that had pre-imposed the fewest conditions of service. We can impose many conditions for going: quality of house and paint, indoor plumbing, absence of snakes, mild climate, a certain degree of health, particular hours of work, equipment, vacations, salaries, pension, and job specifications. When all of our demands are met, then we are ready to respond to the call of God.

The Lord called one family in no uncertain terms to a ministry in Mexico. The husband was a middle echelon executive in the aircraft industry. Their home church had special prayer and sent them out. The Holy Spirit attended that prayer meeting in a powerful way that is rarely experienced. They made their plans for departure. Their split-level house was put up for sale, and they began to pack. However, they put two conditions before the Lord—that they be allowed to move all their furniture into Mexico and that they would get their asking price for the house. The customs officials at the border turned back the Mayflower mover, and though several offers were made for the house, none met their sale conditions exactly. "The Lord evidently is not leading us to this ministry," they reported back to the church, "else he would have met our conditions." Finally, in discouagement, they left the church too. Was it the Lord that did not meet their conditions? Or was it that the Lord called them regardless of their conditions?

When Jesus says in Luke 9:62, "No one who puts his hand to the plow and looks back is fit for the kingdom of God," he is not talking about crushing our love for our family or about homesickness. We would be inhuman if we had none of those feelings on departure. Nor do I think the yearning for rocky road ice cream in Africa's 100-degree heat, or Ruth missing Monday night football is what is meant. The Greek says, "throwing his eyes on the things behind." Throwing his eyes! That is fastening them on the past. A would-be follower crippled by emotional dependency on the things behind will soon resent following. Gone are his or her previous success symbols, various ego boosters, or great plans for continued progress up the ladder of North American or European promotion.

Along with this third obstacle of crippling emotional dependency comes the third command for disciplined following: "Follow with an undivided heart!" A glance over the shoulder to see if the furrow is straight and to remind ourselves from whence we came is different than riding the tractor backwards.

Implicit in these three interchanges with Jesus is also the command to send. When Jesus says "Follow," he also places a demand on the family, friends, and church of the one called. This needs to be clearly understood, for one's individual attempt to follow Jesus can begin in wrenching sorrow when arms that should be supporting are instead clinging, and hands that should be folded in prayer are either turned palm upwards in despair and self-indulgent pity or clenched in anger over having been left. Crippling emotional dependency is as much an obstacle to discipleship for those sending as for those going. Perhaps the wholehearted sending off of a beloved one is how the call to follow Jesus comes to you.

It is easiest for me to picture these three calls to follow in terms of missions because the actual departure to parts unknown most clearly puts into relief the geography of the obstacles they present to discipleship. The call to follow is not only to missions, but it is to mission nevertheless. "You announce the kingdom of God," Jesus replies. "Be fit for service in the kingdom of God," he counsels. This is mission in the broadest sense, a mission in which all Jesus' people are required to participate.

Just as the parables of Jesus are mirrors that reflect one's own image, so these three would-be disciples are meant to be typical of us. Who am I among them? Who are you? I find some of all three in myself. I accumulate foxholes of security and then must leave them again, whether it be a modest bank account or the security of being on a sure salary. I have also had to leave the shaky bird's nest of my self-definition as teacher to a new one of "pastor." But what cover do titles and degrees and properties really give us against the onslaught of the enemy? I also tend to form new crippling emotional attachments to literature, places, and people. Other bonding strengthens me and provides the force in my soul to continue my ministry in Africa.

How about you? You are called, you know. Now. Do not allow the false sense of security given by property and ownership lull you away, or seemingly impossible circumstances cow you, or emotional attachments lure you away. Jesus calls, "Follow me, now; assess the cost and come with all of your heart." You will find new life, indeed, in following him, just as if you were born all over again.